107738

Learning and playing

your child's first years

Learning and playing

your child's first years

EILEEN ELIAS

Pitman Publishing

First published 1972

Sir Isaac Pitman and Sons Ltd
Pitman House, Parker Street, Kingsway, London WC2B 5PB
PO Box 46038, Portal Street, Nairobi, Kenya
Sir Isaac Pitman (Aust) Pty Ltd
Pitman House, Bouverie Street, Carlton, Victoria 3053, Australia
Pitman Publishing Company SA Ltd
PO Box 11231, Johannesburg, South Africa
Pitman Publishing Corporation
6 East 43rd Street, New York, NY 10017, USA
Sir Isaac Pitman (Canada) Ltd
495 Wellington Street West, Toronto 135, Canada
The Copp Clark Publishing Company
517 Wellington Street West, Toronto 135, Canada

£ 29420
124.4
ELI

ISBN: 0 273 31520 X

Text set in 11/12 pt. IBM Baskerville, printed by photolithography,
and bound in Great Britain at The Pitman Press, Bath

Contents

List of plates

*Plates 1 - 3 are reproduced by kind permission of James Galt and Company Limited,
and plates 4 - 8 by kind permission of the Pre-school Playgroups Association
(photographs by D. C. Ranasinghe)*

Jacket photograph by kind permission of James Galt and Company Limited

Learning and playing

your child's first years

How does it work? This young child puzzles it out with a "screwing rod" toy

1
Those first five years

So you've got a baby, and now that the initial period of nervousness is over (most small babies are pretty unnerving at first) you can settle down to enjoy him, or her, for five whole years. Five years lie before you in which to get to know and appreciate that most exciting of all things — a new human personality.

Most young mothers see the pre-school years as stretching into a kind of infinity. It seems impossible that the baby gurgling in his cot, the toddler staggering round the furniture, the three year old with his eternal whys and hows, will ever become a real schoolchild, running off every day at half past eight and not coming home till half past three or four. Yet every older mother will tell you how fast — how very fast — these early years fly. And many teachers, and others who have to do with child development, will also tell you how vitally important they are.

Does it matter what happens to a baby or toddler during the pre-school years? To a young mother it may simply appear that her baby "grows." Yet this very growing, looked at with regard to education, is the important thing. He grows in mind as well as in body; he grows emotionally, too. His growing is really learning, just as his play is really work, to him. Pre-school learning of this kind is the very kernel of education. Indeed it would not be too much to say that parents who can provide the right sort of environment for a child to grow (or learn) to the full during these years, are laying the foundation for his whole future happiness and success.

This is no mere idea; it is a fact, which many recent researches confirm. Dr W. D. Wall, formerly Director of the National Foundation for Educational Research, estimates that as much as fifty per cent of a child's intelligence is fully developed by the age of four, and another thirty per cent by the age of eight. That leaves only twenty per cent to develop during the later school years. So the very first "educator" of all is the family.

Half your child's mental development will be already accomplished by the time you are considering which of the neighbouring primary schools to send him to; his first "teacher" will have been you. Dr Benjamin Fine, a headmaster of a school in New York State, tells the story of a mother who asked a famous child psychologist when she should begin the education of her child, then four years old. Said the learned doctor, "Rush home at once! You have already lost the most important years of your child's life!"

All this sounds rather alarming. But in the deepest sense it is perfectly true. It is what every young mother feels — though she may not realize its full implications — when she cuddles her baby, plays with and talks to her toddler, and establishes a happy, friendly relationship between child and family. Certainly the pre-school child is not "learning" in any formal sense, though as he approaches four or five he may be making a beginning in certain skills. But the mental liveliness and alertness and curiosity, the grasp on life which is what we mean, in a general way, by "intelligence" — this is what his early experiences can help him develop. And it is this positive, forward-looking attitude to living which, as any teacher will tell you, is the groundwork on which later school performance must be based.

Early landmarks

When you look at your new-born baby, and again at that same child one year, two years, or three years later, it is truly amazing what he has "learnt" during even this short time. He is, as a matter of fact, developing at a rate he will never quite equal again. He starts as a tiny babe, helpless, prone, entirely dependent on his mother or on those around him. But at one month from birth, most babies can lift their chins and respond to loud, sudden noises; at two months most can lift their heads up, recognize their mother, and kick fairly vigorously. So just in those eight weeks they have come a long way.

Here are a few further landmarks for which a mother could usefully watch, though it must be remembered that the exact age at which these skills develop varies considerably from child to child. But it is worth observing them, for they form the groundwork which a small child will have to cover before he is

4

ready to enter into easy relationships with other people, or join a playgroup or nursery school:

During the first year he learns gradually to:

> Make noises when talked to.
> Follow moving persons with his eyes.
> Reach for a ring and grasp it.
> Stop crying when talked to.
> Roll from back to stomach and later sit alone, pull himself up and crawl.

During the second year he will learn to:

> Walk alone.
> Say a few words.
> Put bricks in and out of boxes during play.
> Look at pictures shown him in a book.
> Throw a ball.
> Ask for things at table, in some recognizable manner.
> Help a little in dressing and undressing himself.

So by his third birthday your child will already have quite a long list of achievements to his credit, of which the above are only a few. He will also be learning, at his own pace if you teach him wisely without pressure, to be dry and clean, first by day and then by night as well. By about three, most small children are, in these respects, socially acceptable and will only have the occasional "accident."

Another thing to observe and be thankful for is that by three, most children have got over the worst of the temper tantrums and clinging-to-mother fits which assail them during the second year. Someone once called this trying age "the terrible twos," and most mothers will echo this opinion. Three year olds, of course, will still be emotionally turbulent now and then, but because they can now increasingly find an outlet in words and language for their urgent needs, and because they are learning that Mother is a constant figure who doesn't vanish for ever when she is out of sight, they are gradually assuming more control over their feelings and finding ways of adapting to their surroundings, even facing up to new and unexpected situations.

From now on, a child will have other needs, which will show themselves gradually as he matures, and which should be watched for, just as you watched for those early landmarks in babyhood. From three onwards, your toddler will be coming more into contact with other children and other adults, and will be demanding more toys and materials for constructive and experimental play, more scope for his developing imagination, and more freedom to explore his little world, first with one or two other children, later, as he nears school age, with groups sharing his own interests. These needs of his are very real if he is to go on "learning" as he did when you cared for him and played with him in babyhood. They are even more real in the complicated world of today.

It is a strange fact, and one worth pondering on, that though children of three to five are undoubtedly in better physical health than the toddlers of fifty years ago, many of them are just as undoubtedly deprived of things which, in the old days, contributed richly towards pre-school learning. City life may provide many amenities, but the average city street is no longer safe to play in, and town playgrounds, where they exist, are no real substitute for the fields, trees and streams of the country child, or the natural play materials which came the way of young families where father worked at, or near, home, as a craftsman or local tradesman.

Families, too, are smaller; the lively background of Grandma and Grandad, and all the uncles and aunties and cousins who brought continuity and security to the old-style family, has mostly disappeared. Often, the only grown-up a small child sees is his mother, for the whole of the day, except when the milkman calls. Modern homes may be convenient for adults, but a tower flat where the rule of the day is "don't make a noise" or "don't go near the lift," or a housing estate where no ball games are allowed on the grass and there is no place for young children to congregate for adventurous play, can be very frustrating to a normally curious and energetic and exploring under five.

Is all this pre-school learning, though, so very important? Cannot much of it wait until the child starts school and is able to enjoy a richer environment and stimulating teachers? The answer is, from all educationists, a very definite "No." If a child of five is going to make a happy adjustment to school and get the best out of this new environment, he has got to be given, all through the pre-school years, but particularly between three and five, opportunities for experimenting and "finding out." It is too late if we wait until he is five. Even children of approximately equal intelligence, coming into school at five, can differ outstandingly in the way they approach their class-room work or play, according to whether their families have been able to give them the "head start" that is their due. John, who comes into the reception class keen to learn, ready to get along with other children, confident in trying out new skills, will already be ahead of Jane, who has always been "kept quiet," not allowed to make a mess or get untidy, and never mixed with other youngsters in a give-and-take relationship. And this can happen even if John and Jane are of equal intelligence.

Intelligence and environment

Here it might be as well to consider, for a moment, this very vexed question of "intelligence." Is your child bright or dull, or simply average, and, whatever he is, was he born that way, or can he improve or deteriorate in "intelligence"? Many fierce arguments have raged, in the past, over whether intelligence is inborn or not. In our own school-days, the ominous letters I.Q. (intelligence quotient) were bandied about between parents and teachers and local education authorities, especially when children were approaching the age of selection for secondary schooling, and were something of a bogey, particularly to the families concerned. For a long time it was held that a small child's intelligence was fixed at birth, and that it was decided by inherited genes about which parents and teachers could do nothing.

Recent researches have shown, however, that brightness or dullness in children may not be predetermined at birth, and that a child's I.Q. cannot always be tested so accurately as to forecast the whole of his future development. Certainly it would be unrealistic to expect all children, even all those within one family, to be born with an absolutely equal share of what we commonly call "brains." Heredity plays its part. But though certain children may be endowed with more gifts than others, everything depends on the use they make of those gifts. Too many tests have been carried out on too many children for us to dispute that intelligence can flourish or atrophy according to whether it is encouraged in the early days. There has also been the discovery that a child's I.Q. can be raised or lowered by quite a number of points according to the stimulus he receives, especially during the early years.

Most parents, quite naturally, do not want to bother about "testing" their young child's intelligence, whatever I.Q. tests may still be lurking in the future for them at school. Indeed, many people feel that intelligence can never be properly assessed at all, at any age. Recently, there has been much discussion about "creative" intelligence — the kind of open-ended imaginativeness or inventiveness that cannot be measured by filling in blanks in columns of words or juggling with shapes and patterns in the old-fashioned "intelligence test." Many children hitherto underrated in the traditional tests have proved to possess this kind of creativity in a very high degree; the sort of children who later develop marked talents in music, literature and the arts generally, as well as in certain types of scientific thinking.

All the same, we do want to know whether, given as rich an environment as we can provide, our young children are developing as fully as they should. By far the greater number of those entering playgroups and nursery schools and filling our infant class-rooms are of normal intelligence (around 100 I.Q.) and compare favourably with others from similar home backgrounds. But what do you do if you feel that in certain respects your child is not quite like the rest?

A child may be perfectly normal in the sense in which the clinic doctor or health visitor would use the word, yet perhaps you have doubts about him. You are doing all you can to provide him with outlets for his energy, things to play and experiment with, companionship and affectionate mothering, and yet you feel he is not progressing as he should.

There are various reasons for apparent setbacks in young children. Lack of intelligence, wrong environment, absence of affection or stimulus do not account for them; we must look elsewhere. Quite possibly, something has happened in the family circle which has temporarily held up a child's developing powers or dammed back his emotion. Has he been ill? Did he have to go to hospital for a tonsil operation, even though the stay was only for two days? Has the family moved house recently? Have there been tensions between father and mother, or changes of care, a succession of au-pair girls, for instance, all of whom may have loved Sue or Stephen sincerely, but all of whom had different methods of approach to the child in the family?

Very often, the great and moving processes of birth and death, which we have come to accept, profoundly disturb a happy little boy or girl and seem to call a halt to normal development. Progress stops for a while. There are just too many things to cope with. The birth of a baby brother or sister has deep repercussions; it alters a child's place in the family circle, puts new demands on him, wakens old fears and resentments. The death of a grandparent (something we may have been expecting for months or years) comes as a sudden and quite devastating shock to a tiny child who had imagined Grandpa or Grandma would just "always be there." It is little wonder that a child's natural development may be temporarily arrested. Sue's return to bedwetting may be just an unconscious wish to "be like the baby" and regain Mother's anxious care and attention. Stephen's listlessness may be the result of a mind feverishly trying to cope with the mysteries of death to the exclusion of the normal happy activities of a three year old. It is well to try to recognize the cause of these difficulties or stages of arrested development, before we start wondering whether our child is backward or maladjusted or just plain naughty.

There are cases where a child is clearly not developing as he should, in spite of the family's endeavours, or where his behaviour is so upsetting, or so atypical of his age, that advice must be sought. Three or four is not too early an age for help to be offered to a child in such straits as these. The local Child Guidance Service can be contacted by clinic, family doctor or (exceptionally) directly by the parents themselves and really disturbed behaviour or regression should be treated as early as this, for now is the very stage when family attitudes and parental expectations are being set for a child, and when he can so easily be wrongly directed along a path which can only lead to trouble later. Not even the most perceptive teaching at school can put things right if, in the first four years of a child's life, they have really gone seriously wrong.

"Getting through" to your child

By the time a child is three or four, apart from temporary setbacks, he should have become a lively little person and a great companion. He has already mastered the basic skills of getting about, making his wants known, playing with simple toys and responding in a friendly way to other people, his parents and immediate family. He may still go through periods of shyness with strangers, may be quicker, or slower, than some other children in talking, recognizing pictures, or putting puzzles together, or using the equipment in park or playground, but these are only minor variations. By and large, he will be ready for a rather wider world than the four walls of home: more children to play with, more chances for conversation and discussion, more play materials that further his skills and make demands on his ingenuity or imagination. This is the time when parents, alone or in groups, or teachers and staff in nursery schools and classes, are going to be essential educators. The extent to which we can "get through" to the three or four year old and provide for his needs, whether at a nursery group or just at home, will determine the extent to which he will get off to a good start in school at five.

What is the most important way of all to "get through" to your toddler? First and foremost, just enjoy him. Share his activities, be his companion, give to him freely of your time and energy — in short, let these two years between three and five be an enjoyable dialogue between parent and child. This is possible even if you decide to provide him with nursery experience as well. Nursery school or play activities can only supplement, never take the place of, the home, and parents will always be the most important people in the small child's life.

Fathers, quite as much as mothers, are the V.I.P.s of a young child's everyday living, even if they are not always available. (Sometimes, just because of their scarcity value, they may be more important at bedtime than Mother!) I was watching Debbie the other day, curled up on her father's knee, being told a bedtime story. This was not a case of a wailing "Daddy, read me a story" and an irritable "Oh well, just for a minute, but I want my supper." It was a real father and daughter partnership, and I could not tell who was enjoying it more, father or daughter. There was time for leisure, a story to be shared, the comfortable presence of each near the other. I guessed that when it came to Debbie's schooldays, reading for her would be linked, subconsciously, with pleasure: a happy response to something interesting, and therefore invaluable to a later enjoyment of literature.

I saw a similar warm understanding another day in a friend's kitchen, where four-year-old Ian was helping to make pastry. True, his mother would probably have got through her baking morning much more quickly without Ian's helping hand; but Ian, eyes shining, was feeling that he mattered in the world of home, that he too could help, had something to offer, and was learning fast. I knew that when Ian began school, he would be one of those children a teacher soon recognizes as a useful, dependable person, ready to tie shoelaces for a less competent child or give out the milk bottles at break, and, also, a boy with a confident outlook on life, who would not doubt his ability to tackle school work and succeed in it.

Children remember these pleasant shared experiences far longer, and far more deeply, than we suspect. The comfortable feeling of being close to Daddy as he reads, the warm smell of baking day in Mother's kitchen and the excitement of "real cooking," can be knit into the child's life in such a way that they become part of the fabric of home. They help to create that sense of being wanted, trusted and respected, which is a child's greatest incentive and a teacher's most valuable aid.

Second to this — the sheer pleasure of being with your child — I would put the importance of establishing communication lines with him. Communication is the very basis of all education, the passing on of ideas from one person to another. There must be a verbal two-way flow between your child and those about him, not only in these early years, but at school, and indeed throughout his life, with family, friends, teachers, neighbours, employers, and later marriage partners. This process of "getting across" in words must begin while a child is still very young, if it is to become a part of him and be used for what it is, an essential tool for learning.

You might be surprised at the thought that your child's very first venture into communication comes at less than two months of age, with that first smile of recognition. This is the baby's earliest experience of finding a way across to other people. He smiles, and someone smiles back, or laughs, or "answers" in baby talk, and immediately a channel is opened between the baby and his family.

Later, there will be more and better ways of "getting through." Long before your baby can talk, you will be talking to him, sometimes using the age-old baby talk that in the first months seems to come naturally to all mothers, sometimes using real words that, though not understood, yet have meaning of a sort for the baby who listens and enjoys them. Even the youngest child notices the tone of his parents' voices, and responds by chuckling, laughing, and eventually by imitating the sounds they make and experimenting with sounds of his own. The first repetitive, "Da da," "Ma ma," is received with delight, and, finding this happy response, the child goes on to further experiments and imitations till at last he finds language that enables him to communicate.

Talking and singing to your child are vital from babyhood onwards, using speech and song in every kind of way, from baby jingles and finger plays to the lovely rhymes and verses which have been the channel of parent—child communication for centuries. Teachers at school pick out with ease those children who have enjoyed plenty of this exchange of rhyme, song and conversation, whose questions have been answered, who are not afraid to ask the names of things or try to express themselves or describe new experiences. Talk and discussion are the stuff of language, the beginnings of all reading and writing and understanding. So talk to your child about the things that happen during his day, as you work around the house, go for walks, meet interesting things or animals or people, do the shopping. Use the right words for what you talk about for even if a child cannot manage them himself, he will accept them, once the first year of baby talk is over. This is how he learns to build up a vocabulary. It is a great discovery that things have names, that he can ask for something and get it (sometimes), that he can tell his family what he likes and doesn't like, what he wants to do and doesn't want to do and, later, how he feels about situations and people. To be able to put things into words, or have them put into words for him by his family, can immensely ease the minor difficulties of early childhood, as well as merely extending the vocabulary. Most of all, it can help a child see language as a friend rather than an enemy — something he will enjoy at school, as it gradually turns into reading and writing and fills much of his day.

A very small child's talk is bound to be disjointed and scrappy — what someone aptly described as "scribble talk." By the time he is two, he will probably have acquired a vocabulary of some 300 words, and between two and three he will start using short sentences. At about three, he will enjoy looking at picture books and hearing the story told him, so this is the time to introduce him to the books you want him to learn to love. He will soon have his favourites, and perhaps will begin to turn the pages with you, telling you what comes next, or even pretending to read himself.

At three to four, a child will often ask "What does that say?," pointing to letters on cereal packets or to signs above shops or names on garden gates. He may in this way acquire quite a large vocabulary learnt, as it were, the do-it-yourself way. This is the prelude to the reading he will begin at school. He may also try to copy the letters, and ask to be shown how to write his own name — the prelude to writing. But during these pre-school years, for most children at least, it is probably better to concentrate on "how to use words" rather than on "what the letters say." It is quite a help to a teacher if a child can read and write his own name, but it is usually no help at all and possibly a hindrance if his parents have already started him on a formal reading scheme, which may conflict with the one in use at school. Some children, pressed to read too early, find school reading merely boring; they already know it all. Others are made to start all over again — just as frustrating an experience. Most teachers prefer parents, instead, to get the child "ready for reading," by using language for communication so that he understands what words are for, and by providing a rich background of interesting experiences and activities to talk or write about later. It is no use trying to teach a child "to bark at print" like a rather clever puppy, if this is just a mechanical routine which pleases Mother but means nothing.

There are, of course, exceptions to this. A few children just cannot wait to be "taught" to read; they teach themselves, and by four are reading fairly fluently. And it would be foolish deliberately to hold back such a youngster. Fortunately, with today's more flexible infant class-rooms and more individual pace of learning, such a child, if he goes to a suitable school, will probably be allowed to read on his own and not be kept back while the class goes through formal reading drill. It is worth trying to find such a school should you happen to have a very early "self-starter." Children like these usually do much better at a school which is geared to independent learning rather than class teaching, hard though it may be to find.

There is a line of thought, well known to American parents and now to many mothers and fathers in this country, which does actively encourage early teaching of reading — in the nursery, in fact. The American writer, Dr Glenn Doman, has had considerable publicity over here since his book "Teach your Baby to Read" (with its accompanying kit) was first published in Britain in 1965, followed by James Thomson's book on the same subject. Doman, a physiotherapist by training, advocates holding up printed cards before a baby and graduating to specifically prepared books — a method which, he claims, has enabled babies to read as early as two years and three months. In considering such a theory, which certainly appeals to some parents, it is worth remembering that reading, by itself, is only one of a number of skills which the young child likes to try. The question we must ask is, "Is it worth all the effort to teach this particular skill, which a child will acquire anyway as soon as he goes to school?" The moment a youngster gets the feeling that he is doing something particularly clever, or pleasing parents in some special way, by "reading" from printed cards, even if mother makes it into a game, there is a danger that a false emphasis will be put upon reading skill. It is fatally easy for the parent to exert pressure on a very young child without even being aware of the fact, and equally easy for the child to learn to read parrot-fashion "just to please Mother," which is not the function of reading at all. Here it might be worth remembering Dr Spock's words on the "early reader," "Often . . . the parents themselves are more ambitious than they perhaps realize. When he is playing childish games or rough-

housing, they pay only a normal amount of attention. But when
he shows an interest in reading at an early age, their eyes light
up and they help him enthusiastically. The child senses their
delight and responds with greater interest."

Most parents in Great Britain (which starts schooling a year
earlier than the U.S.A.) feel that there are many other more
rewarding things a baby can do than learning word recognition
a full three years before the rest of his age group. There are
definite dangers in trying to choose a child's field of learning
for him instead of letting him choose his own.

If you do want to teach a four year old to read, you might
remember that there are many other methods open to you
besides those of Dr Doman. A look round your public library's
junior department or a chat with his future teacher will put you
on to the track of the various reading schemes already in use for
beginners in this country. There is something to be said, if you
know your local school has big classes and will not have much
time for an individual child, for taking on the job of early
introduction to reading providing you follow the method used
by his future teacher.

Things a young child can do

What other ways are there of fostering the small child's growing
desire to learn and explore? Apart from sharing his interests and
"getting through" to him in conversation and language, there
are certain definite ways of helping him to use his intelligence.
Many psychologists both in Great Britain and in the U.S.A.
consider that one of the best roads to learning is to play at
"sorting" games with your child. Training in sorting and dis-
crimination can be introduced through all kinds of informal
play. Can your child find the differences between things? Try
him with a large button in a box of small ones or a red counter
in a pile of yellow ones. Give him different textures to feel — a
rough piece of wood to compare with a smooth piece of plastic,
a soft bit of velvet to compare with a length of corded ribbon.
He will make these discoveries without any aid from you, and the
exercise of sorting will encourage him to concentrate on a
particular stimulus, and to shift his attention when the principle
of sorting is changed. This is a form of mental agility which will
help him enormously when he goes to school.

Manipulative skills can also be encouraged. Every toddler likes to build and make things, on big or small scales. Give him plenty of materials with which to experiment. A baby will build a tower of bricks just for the pleasure of knocking it down again, but an older child will build constructively and show you proudly what he has made. Later he will use toy cars or farm animals or similar miniature toys, alongside his model or building structure, for more ambitious imaginative games. He will also enjoy building ships and aeroplanes and tractors with large boxes and planks, or will just try out ideas of his own with large-scale constructive "junk." Indeed, "junk" of every kind, large or small, is all grist to his mill; he can see possibilities in it which would never occur to grown-ups. Puzzles and fitting toys, posting boxes, jigsaws, are all fascinating to him, and help him to use eye, hand and brain together. Give him, as well, plenty of scope for "messy" play with clay or plasticine, or a modelling mixture you can make at home out of flour, salt and water. At first he will merely pummel and squeeze these interesting new materials, but before long he will be fashioning small objects like sausages, snakes or birds' nests with eggs inside. This feeling of power over raw material is one of the most satisfying outlets a young child can have. For the same reason, many children, some girls as well as boys, enjoy hammering and simple carpentry. The knowledge that they can fashion things to their pleasure, assert domination over their tools, helps them to gain confidence in a world where they often feel very small and helpless.

Painting is a very valuable activity. Not only does it satisfy a young child's desire to make a mess (a colourful, exciting mess) with wet paint, thick paper and a brush, in a legitimate way, but it also gives an outlet to thoughts, feelings, hopes and fears which a very young child cannot express through speech. Painting is thus a "language" in itself, and often it can tell us more about our own child than we would guess. Newspaper or thick wallpaper and big stubby brushes are useful, and a painting easel gives even more scope than a table or the floor, though either of these will probably get used as well. Indeed, the simplest home-made activities seem to satisfy the child just as much as expensive play material bought from shops. A box filled with sand in the garden, an old motor tyre sunk into the ground to serve as a pool for water play, together with kitchen utensils such as patty pans, colanders, wooden spoons and bits of hosepipe, are just as much enjoyed as "bought" sand-boxes and water tanks. The only exceptions might be one or two really well-made (and therefore fairly expensive) large-scale playthings such as a wooden engine big enough for pushing, pulling and sitting on, or, if it can be managed, a stout and simple climbing frame or garden swing. Just a few of these long-lasting toys, which can be used by several children or passed down a family, are well worth while, even if your child's main stock of play material is of the home-made variety.

Imaginative outlets are very necessary as a child nears school age, for it is now that he wants to imitate and, through play, try to understand some of the situations he is meeting as his world widens. A dressing-up box can be really valuable; filled with bits of lace curtain for brides' dresses, old hats for pirates or cowboys, long skirts for queens' robes, or white aprons for hospital play at doctors and nurses, it can provide real opportunities for acting out the experiences a child dreams about, or enjoys, or even fears. Mother and Father play is also very popular with the four year olds. A Wendy house, even if it is only an old clothes horse draped with curtains, provides a secret place for these domestic games, and will rarely be out of use for long. Dolls and animal toys, household utensils such as pots and pans, brushes and mops, will be brought in here; floors will be scrubbed, imaginary meals cooked on stoves improvised from orange boxes, "children" put to bed in cots — in fact, all the everyday activities of the home will be enacted.

Music is much enjoyed by small children, and if you can buy a triangle, drum or xylophone to supplement the family radio or record player, all kinds of musical games can be played and experiments in sound tried out. A child loves to dance or march to music, and doesn't mind a bit if the "music" you provide is not very professional; many an old piano has been brought into use again when Mother finds the joy her child experiences in moving to music, however sadly her musical skills have deteriorated. Good nursery rhyme (and story) records are published by E.M.I. in their "Playtime" series, whilst the daily radio programme has "Listen with Mother" each afternoon to bring the old favourites, and some new ones, to the child's ear.

Physical outlets are important. Ideally a garden or outdoor space to play in should be a child's right, yet many homes are without much more than a back yard or tiny patio, if that. But even if you have only a long corridor down which a little girl can push her doll's pram, or a boy ride a tricycle, that is at least something. A swing can often be improvised in a doorway, and in a tiny scrap of garden a corner can be found for digging or gardening. For ball play, and the climbing and balancing games children love, you may have to go out to the nearest park or playground; this is one of the greatest problems of our urban communities, and somehow in the near future more outdoor play space will have to be found for the pre-school child to "let off steam" and practise those bodily skills which he will need for his full physical development. Meanwhile, unless we have the luck to live in the country, we must do the best we can by taking small children out to suitable open spaces where they can indulge in active play and generally "let off steam," choosing, if we can, an "adventure" type of playground where the fixed equipment of swings and roundabouts is replaced by the raw materials of adventure logs to climb on and build with, earth to dig, water to dabble in.

A child's first library will have to be considered, too, long before he can read to himself. Building up a collection of books should be a delight to any parent, and those in doubt can consult the local children's librarian, who will allow browsing round the shelves and will probably lend or give a suitable booklet on choosing books for the under sevens. A child's first picture book needs to be well printed on good paper, with clear, gay pictures — not the "scribble" type so many book illustrators imagine children like. It is a good idea to cover books with adhesive transparent film, and to strengthen the spine and corners with adhesive tape. Children give books tough treatment, but this way they can be kept neat and tidy, and train a child in appreciating nicely-cared-for property. Tatty books invite bad handling.

The National Book League gives advice on the choice of children's books, and so does the Children's Book Centre in Kensington, which publishes a bi-monthly review of current literature. Mrs Anne Wood of Aldershot also runs book groups for children, and issues a quarterly publication "Books for your

Children." It is quite fun to make a "home" book for your own child, drawing or pasting in suitable pictures with captions opposite; the child will soon recognize his own family, his house, his pets, the flowers in his garden, and will enjoy "reading" his very own book to visiting aunts and grannies.

Radio, records and TV also supplement story time for many children. Each has its own contribution to make, and if the experience of watching or listening is shared with mother or father, it becomes a real source of interest.

If your child has been lucky enough to enjoy most of these activities, at home or in a group, he will be well prepared for school at five. What other points should you look for when that great day comes? Here is a list of useful practical accomplishments which any infant teacher would appreciate in a newcomer:

> Knowing his own name and address.
> Being able to speak up for himself, especially about using the lavatory.
> Being able, with occasional help, to put on coat and out-door shoes.
> "Managing" in the lavatory, and washing his own face and hands.
> Being able to cope with most foods at table.
> Recognizing his own name or picture on a cupboard door or coat hook.
> Being willing to share toys, wait his turn, and tolerate separation from mother, with just a little help during the first few days.

If your five year old can do most of these things cheerfully and confidently on his first day at school, you will have done a good job of bringing him up during those vital pre-school years.

Who wants taps? A bowl can be just as useful at a pre-school playgroup

2
Nursery school and playgroup

By the time a child is three or four, most mothers will already be realizing that providing all the activities and experiences he needs is a full-time job — and a tiring one at that, particularly if there are other children in the family, or a new baby to be cared for. They will also be realizing that town planners pay more attention in this day and age to where to put the car than where to put the toddler. Most small houses and practically all flats are quite unsuitably designed for all the messy, noisy, adventurous play a young child wants and needs. In addition, long before he meets other children at school, he should be meeting them at play — not just inviting the child next door in to tea, but experiencing the regular shared games and general give and take of a nursery school or playgroup.

Mothers sometimes wonder whether, if there are already other children in the family, nursery schools or playgroups are really essential. Hasn't John already got an older brother to play games with after school, or a little sister to toddle round after him? But ask John what he thinks of big brother, and he'll tell you that someone so much older and stronger is not much fun to play with — always doing things better than himself, or too impatient to play the games he wants. As for baby sister, she's too young to do anything except take up Mother's time, which he wants for himself, and knock down the tower he has so painstakingly built of bricks, or tear up the painting he was keeping to show Daddy.

The fact is that children need others at the same stage as themselves, in order to learn how to take their rightful place in the community. Of course there are exceptions. Not many children of two or two and a half are ready for the social life of a nursery group; not all threes or fours can tolerate long separations from mother, and not all mothers, anyway, agree with the nursery school idea. But on the whole, there is a great and increasing demand for more places in nursery schools, classes or groups, where bigger and better equipment can be made available, more play space provided, and where mothers can gain a breathing space from demanding toddlers. There is nothing wrong in admitting that having to spend every moment of the day with a child at the "when-why-what" stage, and cope with household chores as well, is extremely exhausting. A short daily break from each other usually does both parent and child a lot of good.

People often confuse day nurseries with nursery schools and child minders with playgroups. All cater for small children under five, but in very different ways and with very different purposes in view. Day nurseries are for mothers compelled to go out to work; they take babies as young as six weeks, keep them until school age, and care for them right round the clock, usually from about 7.30 until 5.45, giving them a mid-morning snack, a midday dinner and a high tea. For this, fees are charged, graded according to a parent's capacity to pay. Where a mother is unsupported and can claim help from social security funds, these may be very low. The day nursery aims chiefly to care for the child in the absence of the mother, not merely to supplement normal home life.

A nursery school, however, is chiefly educational; in fact it is a part of our educational system. It keeps the usual infant school hours and holidays, charges no fees (if State maintained), though it does make a charge for meals if these are provided, and is staffed by nursery school teachers assisted by nursery nurses or students. Many schools are part time, taking children mornings or afternoons only so as to allow more to attend; and the age range is from two to five only. The Nursery School Association has been particularly instrumental in pressing for more of these properly staffed and State-sponsored nursery schools.

Child minders and playgroups have one thing in common; they must both be registered with the local health authority and are subject to inspection to ensure that the children cared for are properly supervised and protected. But a child minder in her own home does not usually concern herself with the full programme of nursery school education, though she may provide toys and organized play, and she makes a charge to the parent according to arrangement — how long a child stays, what meals are offered, and so on. A playgroup also is open to inspection by the health authority; in fact it cannot be set up until it has been officially sanctioned by them as suitable. (Note that it does not normally qualify for any financial help from the education authority.) But it is run, often by mothers themselves, for the educational benefit of the children; they are "minded" but they are also given as much experience as possible of nursery school activities, and encouraged to think of themselves as a social group. Hours and fees may vary, as in the case of child minding; but whereas the child minder in her own house takes children of varying ages, primarily for the fees, the playgroup is very seldom a profit-making concern, nor does it expect to take children for most of the day. It may only function once or twice a week, and then perhaps for two or three hours in the morning or afternoon. In brief, it is really a do-it-yourself nursery school, held for the most part in a church hall or club room and taking children mainly over three, to give them at least some experience of nursery life in preparation for school.

Nursery schools

The Education Act of 1944 envisaged, hopefully, a great increase in the number of nursery schools all over the country, counting them as an optional part of educational provision for young children generally. People soon came to realize their enormous value, but unhappily, this part of the Act has never been properly implemented; and as it has always been optional, not incumbent, upon local authorities to provide such schools where they are desired by parents, there is still, and is likely to be for some years, a most serious shortage of them. In fact for the past ten years or so, there has been a ban on new nursery school building by local authorities, and only now is this being lifted under special circumstances, as for instance, in certain educational priority areas in the big cities. Only a very tiny proportion of threes to fives can be accommodated in State nursery schools — which is largely why the playgroup movement has gone forward with such impetus. If the State cannot or will not do it for us, these mothers say, we will do it ourselves; and in the majority of cases such groups work well, though they may have to limit their equipment if they are run on a shoestring budget.

If you would like to get your child enrolled at a State nursery school, where you know the teachers will be trained and the equipment will be rich and varied, then you should put down his name at the earliest opportunity. All have enormous waiting lists; but there are special circumstances worth noting, which may hasten your child's entry. A doctor or health visitor can recommend nursery education for a child whose development is being seriously impeded by, say, illness in the family, a home shared with "difficult" relatives, or behaviour problems which are likely to respond to daily mixing with other children in an attractive environment. If this is the case in your home, then it would be worth enlisting medical support. There are "priority" places which are sometimes kept for children whose need is urgent.

Otherwise, the best you can do is to find out the where-abouts of your local nursery school (the Education Office will tell you) and see that your child's name is duly given a place on the list.

What will his day be like if he is lucky enough to attend a State nursery school? You can be sure he will be in good hands, for the head teacher and staff will be college trained, and understand your toddler's needs. One thing you may be misled about — it is not a "school" in the sense of a place where a child is taught lessons or made to sit at a desk or table. He may, indeed, as he nears five, be helped through play to make a beginning — counting the spoons and forks at the dinner table, weighing and measuring sand and water, tracing big letters round templates or in sand, perhaps writing his own name and learning to recognize it above his peg in the cloakroom. But the aim of nursery school is free but purposeful play, coupled with the experience of joining with others in interesting activities such as singing games or listening to a story. There will be no pressure on a child either to do what he is not ready for, or to join a group unless he wishes to, though every encouragement will be given him to increase confidence and enjoy social mixing.

A nursery school usually has one or two big playrooms, with

child-sized chairs, benches and tables easily moved about, and plenty of floor space. Toys will be easy for a child to get out and put away himself, and there should be a large variety of equipment. There will also be outdoor play space, with opportunities for climbing, swinging, sliding down a chute, perhaps paddling, certainly a sandpit and water tank, and boxes and planks for "making" things and thus learning to negotiate steps, seesaws and balancing on narrow ledges — the sort of outdoor activities children love. There will almost certainly be pets to be watched and taken care of, a "library" corner somewhere, and a "home" corner for mother and father play. And there will be plenty of shared games and music — perhaps a band. Mornings often start with a short period of "letting off steam," after which children gather in a ring for "news time" or just to make friends and talk together with their teacher, or show off little treasures like picture postcards brought from home. Part-time nursery schools will have a mid-morning or mid-afternoon break for orange juice or milk and perhaps a biscuit or apple, and whole-day nurseries will have a dinner hour preceded by toileting and washing in the cloakroom, and an afternoon rest on low beds, or rugs in the garden. Most full-time nursery schools like parents to fetch their children between three and half past, so that there is still plenty of time for a toddler to enjoy his mother's company during the afternoon, or go to meet an older brother or sister from school.

A nursery school is specially adapted to a young child's needs, so you will find that the cloakrooms have child-sized washbasins and toilets, and the toy shelves are low enough for a child to manage unaided. Coat pegs will be labelled with his own special picture, so that he can easily recognize his symbol. The same symbol will recur on his face flannel, toothbrush and towel, if he stays all day and needs these things. The purpose of all this is to develop his independence, so that by the time he reaches school at five he will be able to manage for himself in all these personal details. Children learn very quickly when they see others doing the same things, and a boy or girl who has "battles" at home over teeth cleaning or toileting is very unlikely to continue such behaviour at nursery school, where daily routines are fun. Similarly, a boy or girl who is finicky over food at home generally eats cheerfully like everybody else at the nursery school dinner table. This is yet another valuable reason for trying to get a "difficult" child into a nursery school; it saves so much wear and tear on the nerves at home!

Taking part in the life of the community is another useful lesson for the three or four year old. Helping arrange the flowers set the dinner table, put out or clear away the low beds, fold the rugs, get out the balls for a garden game or tidy away the musical instruments after a "band" session, he feels himself a part of the group. All this can be done to some extent at home, but it is much easier for a child to develop a sense of responsibility at nursery school, where he takes his turn with other children at keeping the place tidy and "doing the chores."

Most nursery schools realize that the first days away from Mother, even for a few hours only, are something of a shock to a young child; and most head teachers allow a gentle approach, with Mother staying a while to settle in her child, until he feels safe enough to watch, and ultimately join in with, what others are doing. Slipping away in the hope that he "won't notice" is not a good idea; but neither is it helpful to stay too long and pay too much attention to him. Usually it takes a day or two for a child to feel really secure at nursery school, and in a few cases it simply does not work, and the best thing to do is to drop the idea and try it again a little later on, when the child is just that bit more mature. But most soon begin to play naturally, first with one or two specially inviting toys, later perhaps with a friend, finally, and quite cheerfully, joining a group. And it is very rare indeed to find a child who, after a term at nursery school, is not an extremely happy and busy little person, quite reluctant when the weekend comes and there is "nobody to play with."

There are also nursery classes, run on the same lines as nursery schools, attached to certain primary schools in various parts of the country. These come under the general surveillance of the infant school head teacher, but they are staffed by nursery-trained teachers and usually take children in the year previous to school entry. Here again, you would be well advised to enter your child's name early, as places are greatly in demand. The nursery class may be in a separate building, or it may be attached to the infant school, but the children in it will, to a certain extent, be kept apart from the rough-and-tumble of the ordinary school playground, and will receive the same nursery education as in a separate nursery school.

Choosing a private nursery school

If you want an independent nursery school, you will have to be prepared to pay fees, which vary, and which can be very high. Naturally, the more you pay, the more you should be able to expect in the way of staffing, space and equipment, and a very cheaply run nursery school should be viewed with considerable caution. Fees range widely, from around £2 to £35 a term, according to hours and provision. Some function only for two hours on one or two days a week; others may take children for a full day, with meals as well. They must all be registered under the Nurseries and Child Minders Act, so you can be fairly sure that the staffing ratio is adequate and the premises safe for children's play; but it is the quality of staffing and play materials that matter, and these you must assess for yourself. Visit the nursery school when the children are there, and watch how they are handled, and what pressures are exerted on them: occasionally a nursery school is more of a "school" than a "nursery" and is viewed chiefly from the point of view of a child's "getting on," which is not the true purpose of this stage in education. You alone know your child and his needs, and it is important to feel that he is in the hands of people who understand him, who will give the necessary framework of control to a lively youngster, be gentle with a timid one, or supply the rich material for exploration and play needed by the gifted.

All nursery schools, maintained or independent, should work hand in hand with the family, as an extension of home life, not as a substitute for it. To this end it is important that parents are welcomed, encouraged to chat with the teachers when they come with their children, and to help actively in various ways — sewing aprons for painting sessions, mending toys, contributing old clothes for the dressing-up box. One London State nursery school I know regularly arranges a seaside outing when mothers join their children on a coach trip to the coast, and this is eagerly looked forward to by staff, children and parents alike. A good private nursery school will have the same close links with the children's families, and also with the surrounding community. A useful way of forming an impression, when choosing a private nursery school, is to ask what these links are. Does the school encourage visitors? Do nursery students from the local Further Education College take an interest in it, and visit it as part of their studies? (They usually do this where there is a State nursery school within reach, as a matter of course.) One private nursery school I have visited invites senior girls from the nearby secondary school to go regularly once a week and play with the children as part of their social studies course. The same one encourages its children to sing carols and take Christmas gifts to an old people's home, as their part in the life of the neighbourhood. All these might be good pointers towards choosing a well run private nursery school. You might also ask the head teacher of your local primary school, who often has personal knowledge of private establishments in the district; and of course, a list of independent pre-school provision is always kept at your local Health or Education Office.

Playgroups and their purpose

If there are no pre-school facilities, either State or private, on the scale of a proper nursery school or class, your child still need not be denied nursery experience altogether. This is where the rapidly growing playgroup movement comes in. A playgroup is simply a small group of under fives, usually over three, who meet for part of the day under the care of a leader and her helpers; perhaps daily, possibly only once or twice a week. These informal but very useful groups are the parents' answer to the extreme shortage of nursery schools. They owe their origin to the work of devoted mothers who are prepared themselves to provide, as far as they can, what the State denies them.

You can find out about playgroups by asking other mothers, or the Health Visitor at the clinic; by enquiring at your town hall, health or education office; or by watching the local press, or newsagents' windows or community centres' notice boards, which often carry details of local groups already organized or of mothers wishing to form one. But undoubtedly the best way is by personal recommendation; for the provisions these groups make vary so greatly that you need to know quite a lot about them before choosing one for your child.

Playgroups are sometimes run by mothers on a rota basis, or sometimes by a professional worker with children — an ex-teacher, a married nursery nurse with time to spare, or some-one else with specialized knowledge, assisted by students, or mothers. It is far better to choose a group where at least one of the staff is either very experienced with small children, or possesses some qualification. But the fact that mothers are usually helpers adds a very special flavour to these groups; and indeed you may soon find yourself on the rota of parents prepared to take an active part in running the group.

Let us take a look at the business of running a local play-group; for it is quite possible to initiate one yourself if you can get sufficient support. But it is important not to enter into such an experience lightly, or without studying what is involved; for looking after other people's small children is very different from looking after your own.

If you contemplate starting your own playgroup, a great deal of help can be obtained by joining the Pre-school Play-groups Association, which exists to further the establishment of such groups and to advise in all sorts of ways, from suggesting activities to getting discount on play materials and arranging insurance (a "must" where the care of other people's children is concerned). The Association will give you the name of its nearest honorary organizer, and publishes a stimulating magazine written specially for its members.

How do you set about things? The first thing to do is to find a like-minded group of mothers. It is important that the people concerned get on with each other, share (roughly) the same views about the bringing up of children, and be absolutely reliable in the matter of turning up when their services are needed.

Ideally, a "playgroup mother" should be a warm, under-standing type of person, not easily "flappable," with kind but firm control of young children and an inventive and flexible mind. This last is particularly important. In a playgroup, unless you have a qualified person in charge, mothers will have to devise their own programmes, which will often entail dealing with all sorts of emergencies, from toddlers crying for Mummy to those trying to climb over the garden gate or tumbling down steps and bumping their noses, and at the same time keeping other children occupied and happy at all sorts of busy pursuits. It is this ever-changing pattern of young children's daily activities which presents the challenge to a playgroup leader. A trained person will know how to adapt to varying situations; an ordinary mother will have to be imaginative and ingenious enough to cope.

Another thing which must be considered in choosing staff is the time factor. "Playgroup hours are from nine to twelve" sounds simple enough; but what it really means is arriving at eight thirty, and getting equipment out, and at the other end, tidying everything away, and waiting for the last lingering parent to come and fetch Tom or Sally. This may not be so difficult if the group is run in somebody's home, but few houses have sufficient space to accommodate the numbers needed to make a playgroup worthwhile, and the usual procedure is to rent a church hall or similar premises, which will entail packing and storing away every bit of equipment, both indoors and out, with consequent demands on the staff's time.

How many helpers will be needed? The exact ratio will depend upon local regulations, but most groups find that at least one to each eight children is needed (with a minimum of two helpers), unless one of the staff has special qualifications such as a nursery nurse's certificate. For a group of about twenty, which is a manageable size allowing for the fact that some children will be absent on various days, you would need, probably, two staff, plus an extra helper, a young girl or one of the mothers, who would come on a rota basis, besides some "reserves" for emergencies. So, taken all in all, quite a number of people would be involved in the actual running of the group, apart from those who do the paper work, mending of toys and so on.

Premises and equipment

It is essential, before getting started or even making definite plans, to be sure you are complying with official regulations for the minding of children for payment (and fees must be asked if you are to buy equipment, hire premises and pay even a token salary to helpers). This means writing to the Medical Officer of Health and asking for a list of his requirements for starting a group under the Nurseries and Child Minders Act. Official inspection must be made of premises, staffing, safety pre-cautions and other necessities; and only after you have found premises and staff and had these approved by the M.o.H., the Planning Committee and the Fire Officer for your district, will you be able to start.

Where to hold your group is a tricky question — often the hardest part of the whole procedure. Spacious old houses, vicarages with big gardens, private homes with large ground-floor rooms and outdoor play facilities, are hard to come by, though where they exist, they offer, perhaps, the friendliest and homeliest environment of all to small children. Church halls, welfare centres, scout or guide huts, youth clubs, sports pavilions, are other possibilities; but it will probably take time to find these, agree on a realistic rent, come to terms with a caretaker who may not at first take kindly to the idea of small children about the place, and modify the cloakroom and garden facilities for the use of toddlers. Storage for toys, accessibility for parents bringing children by car or bus, proper heating facilities, lavatories and washbasins that can be made small enough for children's use (often just by putting a wooden box beneath them to act as a step) — all these must be considered. And the rent must be within your budget; if you are charging, say, from 12½p to 25p per child for each session, buying equipment and paying a small salary to staff, it is clear that this item must not be too high.

It is worth noting that there are circumstances under which a grant may be payable to your playgroup. Conditions for this vary greatly — on whether, for instance, your staff all happen to be qualified — but it is always worth the enquiry. Grants are more easily obtained if your group is being run by a properly constituted committee, so that it comes under the heading of a charity and gains relief from income tax and selective employ-ment tax. Advice on drawing up such a constitution is one of the services which the Pre-school Playgroups Association provides.

Fitting out a playgroup, once consent has been obtained, is an interesting job — though it will rarely cost you less than £50 to begin with. Fund-raising activities can start you off; people are usually well disposed towards playgroups, and local Residents' Associations, public bodies and even industrial concerns showing goodwill to children can be approached for financial help. Coffee mornings and jumble sales can also bring in useful small amounts; or an appeal in the local newspaper might bring rewards.

Parents will probably be ready to assist with offers of children's toys and books; and sometimes the library will lend a collection of books from time to time. Another source of equipment about which not all parents know is the Education Office, which occasionally has "used" small furniture for sale which handy fathers can paint.

Shops and factories often have waste materials which any playgroup would be glad to have. Odd bits of wallpaper, newsprint, cardboard boxes or cartons, polystyrene oddments, pieces of material from dressmaking establishments, or offcuts of wood from a timber yard for sanding down to use as building bricks, or for children's carpentry — all these are invaluable. Big toys are harder to come by, but there are families with older children who are willing sometimes to part with discarded tricycles, scooters, dolls' prams, or even garden paddling pools or swings. All of these will need careful vetting to make sure they are safe for children's use.

If you are in doubt about what to buy, beg or borrow, there are educational supply firms whose catalogues will give you useful ideas. Firms like Galt's, Abbatt's, the Educational Supply Association, or Playcraft issue catalogues full of equipment. An interested infant school head teacher might also allow you to "sit in" one morning while her children are playing, and watch quietly which materials are the most popular and give the best value. This will help when deciding priorities on your limited budget.

Toys and materials need to be as varied as possible. Obviously you cannot provide everything a full-scale, fully subsidized nursery school would offer, but at least you can cater for broad areas of children's interests. Some quiet individual occupations will be needed: paints, scissors and paper, jigsaws, picture books, and constructional toys. Some group materials — dolls and their bedding, household playthings to use in a "home" corner, a toy telephone, miniature cars and farm animals to use with building blocks — will encourage several children to play together. Imagination can be stimulated with dressing-up clothes or glove puppets; outdoor play encouraged by the provision of some big garden toys. Sand and water in some form are a "must," and clay, if kept under a damp cloth in a tin and used on boards, need not prove too messy. And for gathering the children together with an adult in charge, books for reading aloud, and musical instruments, will be great assets.

One final necessity is a first-aid box, for you never know what small children will get up to; indeed, it is useful to have someone on the staff who has had first-aid training. A doctor's phone number kept handy, and notes on each child, including not only name and address and mother's telephone number but a few facts about past illnesses or health requirements, will also help to avoid worries or panic. It is worth organizing these details so that you can then feel free to spend your time with the children, without worrying if Robert's snuffles are going to turn to measles, or whether one of Pat's frequent tumbles will one day need a stitch from a doctor who may be difficult to contact.

Playgroup problems

Children coming into a playgroup for the first time need plenty of supervision. Some, from restricted homes, will merely rush about for the first few sessions; this is quite understandable, and they will need time to settle down to quieter occupations. Others may have been used to a great deal of individual attention from mother, and will soon get bored and naughty if they are not immediately found interesting things to do.

Children will need to learn social behaviour — not to throw tantrums, not to snatch toys, not to demand adult attention all the time. Sometimes the latter is particularly difficult to learn when a child's own mother is amongst the helpers, and allowances will have to be made for this.

One great help is to attend classes or lectures, where these are available, on child psychology or playgroup management. The number of these is yearly increasing. You can ask at your local Further Education College whether there are facilities, and if you can make up a group and find a tutor, then there may be a good chance of getting one started in districts where no such provision is made. The Pre-school Playgroups Association runs training courses, too, and tries to provide a playgroup for the children of those mothers who attend them. Radio and TV programmes, also, often deal with the subject of young children and their needs; and there are one or two correspondence courses in playgroup technique, notably the "Playgroups Course" run by the National Extension College at Cambridge.

Problems sometimes arise amongst the staff themselves. Working in a team is not easy, and there are sure to be questions which need sorting out. In this matter you will need to decide the role each individual is to play, whether as leader, assistant, helper with the younger ones or with the older children, or clerical worker; there will be plenty of paper work, as well as the need for a treasurer to manage the money side of things. Any special talent should be utilized, even if it is not "professional" in the accepted sense; children love someone who can play the piano, but they won't worry if the playing is not very good! Someone with a good voice and manner for telling stories is worth her weight in gold, and can often pull a troublesome group of children together on a wet day when things tend to get out of hand. And there is scope also for the "ordinary" mum who will wash paint pots, put out fresh paper for painting, clean up sticky paste boards, sweep up woodwork shavings, or get ready the beakers for the morning drink.

It takes time to get such a group smoothly running, and utilize the various skills and enthusiasms people have to offer; but in spite of bad days and awkward moments, running a play-group, once you get absorbed in it, can be tremendous fun, and prove a very worth-while job in providing nursery experience for children who would not otherwise have it.

Helping your child to mix

Supposing it is totally impossible to get your toddler into a nursery school, class or playgroup — is there any other form of organized companionship he can enjoy? You should certainly not be dissuaded from looking around to see whether any similar activities are provided for small children in your district, even if these are only on an occasional basis.

Few places are without a local park, playground or village playing field, and if you can do nothing else, you can at least take John or Susan "down to the swings" to meet other children from the neighbourhood, and other mothers with whom you can make friends. Even on such a small scale, children can learn to take turns on the roundabout, join in a ball game, or share a tricycle. A ball or a skipping rope taken along with you will serve as an invitation to others to play. You cannot just leave small children there by themselves to organize their own games, for parks and playgrounds attract older ones as well as tinies, and the younger children can get bullied or knocked down or simply pushed aside from swings or seesaws. But gradually a child will feel his way into the group, with mother there in the background to keep an eye on things.

Some blocks of flats have their own playgrounds, but a small child cannot be left alone there unless there is proper supervision. (I have seen broken bottles in children's sandpits, and watched small boys run into the road after a ball where such a playground is not securely fenced in.) But many London parks, and some in other parts of the country, have play space for toddlers, with skilled attendants. London children have extensive provision in the One o'Clock Clubs, where mothers can bring pre-schoolers each afternoon and relax nearby while the children play under trained leadership, in the open, or in huts if the weather is wet. These are also very valuable meeting places for the mothers themselves to enjoy a pleasant hour or two with the minimum supervision of their children.

In summer, the swimming pools often have paddling places where toddlers can find shallow water, and even little beaches, stepping stones and waterfalls, to play in while their mothers relax. This again helps children to mix and learn to join in group activities — making a dam with sand, or constructing a deep pool with a bridge of stones across it — though of course they will have to be watched whenever they play in water. One children's pool I know has a concrete "boat" in the middle of it, and also a "castle" on which children love to climb. A summer day at the paddling pool, with another young family and a picnic basket, can give your toddler a great deal of experience in meeting and getting along with other children.

Libraries often have story hours for the under fives, when a special children's librarian gathers a group round her once or twice a week, and reads or tells a story to them for about twenty minutes. During this time, mothers can sometimes slip away and do some quick shopping, getting their children used to being left with other adults. One library I visited, which was next door to the welfare clinic, arranged its story hours to coincide with the "clinic" days, so that toddlers could be entertained while Mother popped next door with the baby.

There is even a move now to provide "shopping crêches" where children can be left for an hour or two at a very moderate charge whilst parents go off to the local shopping centre. One of these, which I visited recently, had been running for a number of years, and though there was no formal register, and parents could just drop their children in at any time on market days, the same ones seemed to gather each week so that the effect was much the same as at a regular play group. In the same town, a crêche is held at the local hospital, mainly for under fives whose mothers are working on the nursing or domestic staff; but it is flexibly run, so that young children accompanying their parents on visits to relatives in hospital, or going regularly with mother to the ante-natal clinic when a new baby is on the way, are also integrated for short periods into the group. Even this brief experience of shared play and meeting new adults has proved of value in getting small children to take the first step forward into the community.

Much more of this imaginative, flexible approach to play provision for under fives is needed in our towns and cities, and also in rural districts as well, where, though there may be more play space, children are often isolated and have fewer opportunities for forming regular playgroups due to transport difficulties.

But most of all, pre-school provision is needed for the tower-flat dwellers, whose number is rapidly increasing, and whose opportunities for mixing with other children are becoming fewer, as flats rise higher and playgrounds are further and further out of reach. Someone has aptly called these children in twenty-storey flats, "prisoners in the sky." Their mothers cannot take them down continually to ground-floor play space unless it is well supervised, and even then the distance for a toddler in an outdoor playground looking up to a mother on the twentieth storey balcony must seem enormous and

insuperable. There are ways and means of building nursery
provision within the blocks themselves, perhaps on every other
floor; or for aerial "corridors" crossing from building to
building, which would at least enable dolls' prams to be pushed,
tricycles to be ridden, and mothers to meet and chat. On
housing estates, too, there is a trend towards providing "play
flats" or "toddlers' centres" where children can be kept happy
and busy under skilled supervision. The Save the Children Fund
were amongst the first to try to provide nursery experience in
the most densely populated urban areas, albeit they had to
manage on a shoe-string budget and often in difficult premises.
But children of all social classes and all kinds of home background really need adequate nursery school or playgroup
facilities — not as a substitute for the home, or a palliative for
poor housing conditions, but as part of their educational right.

In the meantime, there is quite a lot that an ordinary mother
can do, with the help of other parents similarly placed. Pressure
for more nursery schools and classes, pressure for more playgroup and child development courses for interested parents,
more experiments in playgroups of every kind, more imaginative approaches to child care for busy mothers in shops,
markets, or hospital waiting rooms, all help to arouse public
consciousness of the need of the young child to bridge the gap
between himself and the world of school, soon to be entered.

A busy morning "making things" at a pre-school playgroup

3

First days at infant school

What kind of first school will your child be going to? This is an important choice for most parents, and certainly should not be left till the last moment. Naturally, if your nearest infant school is a good one, and you already have happy relations with it through older children, or friends whose families attend it, your choice will be easy. There is no point in a five year old's travelling a long distance to school if he could be just as well served round the corner.

However, parents in fact do have a wider range of selection than many of them imagine, and since a child's first experience of school is likely to affect the whole of his future happiness and learning capacity, it is well worth "shopping around," if this is possible, for the one most suited to him. Children differ greatly, and what suits your neighbour's young Peter may not be at all suitable for your own little Sheila, even if the school recommended is good of its kind. Then, too, different parents want different things for their young: if academic results are all-important to the Smiths, they may matter very little to the Joneses across the road. You alone have the ultimate responsibility for trying to find the best for your child.

Many parents have their choice restricted owing to the "zoning" system, which operates where too many children want to attend the same school. This is not a legal arrangement; it is merely a local head teacher's policy; but it does work against parental choice, since you may find that one school to which you apply for a place cannot grant it to your child because you live in the wrong "catchment area," or district from which that particular school population is drawn.

It sometimes puzzles parents that a boy from down the road may be accepted in a school outside the local "zone" whereas their own son, only a few doors away, is told he must go to the one in his own area. This is not just a head teacher's favouritism, however much it looks like it when you are smarting under apparent injustice. It simply means that the head teacher, at the time the other family applied, did happen to have a place available — perhaps owing to another family's removal from the district. But now that place has been filled. It is only common sense for teachers to try to restrict entry where one waiting list goes back, say, four years and another waiting list is practically non-existent. There is no doubt that the new, modern, attractively sited school with the nice young staff will get more applicants than the older one in a less fashionable area. And the staff obviously have to "zone" to some degree.

What are the reasons which might allow you to choose a school outside your "zone?" If you are familiar with them, you can make out a good case for your application, even if it calls for a certain amount of persistence. One is that older brothers or sisters already attend that school; this would clearly make it easier and pleasanter for a younger one to attend there too. Another fair reason might be based on transport considerations, or dangerous road crossings. Or, of course, if you yourself are a teacher, it is obviously simpler for you to take your own five year old to school with you, or to one near yours, even if it is not the school in your immediate "zone."

Religious reasons are also acceptable. Roman Catholics want to send their children to R.C. schools, and parents wishing their children to be brought up in the Church of England faith may reasonably prefer them to attend a Church school. (It is less likely that permission would be given to, say, a humanist who did not wish his child to be taught in the local Church school; but again, it is worth trying.)

Parents who have strong concerns of their own about such things as corporal punishment, or those who are very much opposed to "streaming," could also bring these arguments to bear on the local schooling situation. Their case might or might not be allowed by the Education Officer who decides these things, but again, persistence may work wonders. Places, however, are very rarely allotted to children outside the local authority boundary; and where the school asked for involves increased travel expense, parents may be required to meet this themselves.

Choosing a first school

Where there is more than one infant school in your district —
and there may be two or three available — what should you look
for? First. do not be influenced too much by outward appearance.
New and shining schools in modern districts may have much to
offer, but the stretches of beautiful green grass outside, and the
attractive entrance hall with its flowers, do not automatically
mean that the education inside is better than it is in the old
type of school to which fewer parents send their children. In
fact, in some cases, the old school, if it has been remodelled on
imaginative lines by a progressive head teacher, may, in spite of
its grim exterior, actually have more space and smaller classes
than the school which is so popular because it is new. One
London primary school in a very unattractive area is, nevertheless, better off than its newer neighbour because it has two halls,
wider corridors which offer more room for children's activities,
and a hut for arts and crafts built in the playground. It also has
one or two spare class-rooms which have been turned into
"centres" for maths and science, and for library work, and space
where parents can come and do odd jobs like sewing or covering
books for the school. Other schools, not so far away, are more
modern and pleasant, but so crowded that they actually have
less to offer. "Ours is one of those tall buildings that stick out
like a sore thumb against the skyline," says its headmaster, "but
it's what goes on inside that matters."

What goes on inside is what you have got to find out when
making a choice. And this is really entirely due to the
personality and ideas of the head. It is the head and the staff
who "make" the atmosphere of a school, particularly a primary
school, so it is the head whom you should make a point of
meeting, somehow, before you decide between one school and
another.

Often it is possible to write, briefly, beforehand, asking
whether a head teacher will see you to discuss the entry of your
child to the school. If so, then you can go, prepared mentally
with a list of questions you want to ask, and you may be invited
to look round the school first and then have a chat with the
head. If you are not prepared, you may find that you go away
not having learned what you really wanted to know; you may

hear about examination successes in the junior school, and still not have met the head of the infant department where your five year old will start. (Many infant departments are attached to, or part of, a larger primary school, and it is the head of the primary school whom you will meet.)

Or you may know what the "uniform" is, if it exists, and what games the children play, but still not be sure what reading methods are taught, or whether five and six year olds get smacked when they are naughty. What is important is to assess the general atmosphere into which your child will go on his first day, and to meet, if you possibly can, some of the teachers who will handle him. The personality of the staff, the methods of teaching, and the attitude to discipline, are far more important than "successes" further up the school, games results or uniforms.

If a head cannot see you personally, then you may be able to visit two or three schools on occasions like jumble sales, or Open Days. Here, at least the school will be open for you to look around, and you can form your own impressions. Still another way of assessing a school's "tone" is by talking to parents meeting their children at the school gates, and by watching the children as they come out. You will learn a lot about what goes on inside by observing this meeting between parents and children, and listening to remarks made.

Two types of schools

In general, you will notice that there are two basic types of primary schools, with of course many compromises and variations in between. But there is a clearly discernible difference between the "feel" of a formal school and that of a progressive one based on the latest research about how children learn. In a formal school, the place will probably be quiet and orderly; children (if you go in school hours) will be working in class-rooms behind closed doors, and glances through windows will be likely to show you rows of desks, teacher and blackboard in front, and, apparently, everyone in the class engaged on the same type of work: all doing painting together, or all reading from the same book, or listening to the teacher.

The materials used may be very good indeed; well kept reading books, well written exercise books, practical equipment

for mathematics, a tidy nature table, and notices in neat handwriting pinned to walls or boards. The head may be welcoming,
obviously conscientious, and will appear to have the children
under good control. There will probably be a detailed timetable
in the head's study, where you can see at a glance what is going
on from day to day in the various class-rooms or in the school
hall or gym. Children walking about the building will be doing
so quietly, possibly in lines, and there will be little or no
talking in the class-rooms and no groups of pupils working
together or helping each other; equally, there may be incomplete
attention to what the teacher is saying, and usually there will
be at least one or two children looking out of the window or
idly "doodling" in an exercise book because they are not
interested in what the lesson is about.

In the other type of school, it may be quite difficult to find
the head at all. He or she will probably be in amongst the
children somewhere, either working with a small group or just
wandering round seeing what is going on. It may even be difficult to find the class-rooms; for in some of the most progressive
schools there are few, if any, barriers between "rooms," and
the place is run on an open plan, with "home bays" instead of
class-rooms and "resources areas" in which pupils gather to get
on with some pursuit. As for finding the teacher, she too may
not be where you would expect — in front of a class — but
sitting at a bench or table working alongside the children,
helping them stick pictures on a frieze, examining tadpoles in a
jar, answering questions about an experiment with a candle and
a flame and a bottle, or suggesting how best to cut out wallpaper
to fit the dimensions of the dolls' house. If the school, as so
many of these are, is run on "family grouping" lines, you may
find children of various ages sharing the same area; fives to
sevens together, in the infant department, just as eights, nines
and tens may be together in the junior section. And if there is
"team teaching," children may be working, not with one class
teacher only, but with a number of teachers, so that it is difficult
to know where one "class" begins and another ends, especially
as there may be many activities — modelling, play-making,
mathematics, needlework, music, reading — all going on together.
The impression you will get will be very much like that at a
nursery school, except that the children will be doing quite

advanced work; they will certainly be so engrossed that they will rarely bother to stop what they are doing and notice a visitor.

Between these extremes, of course, there are many variations. Some schools still have staff, or heads, who prefer the formal type of education — every child in the class doing the same thing at the same time — and even though other teachers favour freer methods, a compromise will be the only possible situation. Many schools have fairly formal lessons in the morning, but leave afternoons free for children to make their own choice of what to do. Many have time-tables but these may not be at all detailed, leaving large chunks of time in which each teacher can follow whatever pursuit best fits in with the children's current interests. There will still be arithmetic, writing, reading, music, but the subject will probably not change just because the bell rings; if the children want to go on, they may.

Children may still be seen walking round school or play-ground in lines, but conversation will be allowed; and it will probably be a child who shows you round the school, not a teacher. There may still be class-rooms and separate teachers for each age group, but within those class-rooms, pupils may be working in smaller groups, and the more able may be helping the less confident.

All these are degrees of formality or informality; and much will depend on the age and attitude of the teachers. Before visiting any school, then, it is well to have some impression of the two types of schools and their purposes: one will teach through fairly formal methods, expect traditional discipline, and probably classify pupils at some point in their primary career as A, B or C (streaming); the other will have abandoned streaming, will let the children, as it were, "teach themselves" through discovery methods, and will keep control without any apparent "discipline" of the punishment type. How far you want to go along one line or the other depends on what you yourself think is the purpose of education — whether the child's mind is, as a teacher once said, "a well to be filled, or a fire to be kindled." You will also know your own child from the past five years, and have already formed some opinion of the educational "climate" under which he seems to flourish best.

Some parents would like a less formal first school for their child, but worry about what will happen when he is seven or

eight and has to go "up to the juniors." If the junior department is run along the same free lines, will John "get on" as well
as James next door, who does traditional sums, spells correctly,
writes a good hand, and generally seems in advance of John?
There has been much discussion about this facet of "free"
schooling, especially when the informal approach is continued
into the junior school, where many parents feel children really
ought to be getting down to work — especially if there is an
examination in view.

In fact, research supports the conclusion that where children
are encouraged to go at their own pace and choose their activities, getting help from their group rather than "waiting for
teacher to come round," there is actually more scope both for
the bright child to get ahead, and for the slower to receive the
teacher's individual attention. Certainly, in many of the "free"
type of schools I have visited, where this approach has been
carried up from the infants through to the juniors, the standard
of written work has been remarkably high in the older groups;
even without the stimulus of "marks" and "places in class,"
children have been anxious to improve their own standards,
competing not against others but against themselves and taking
pride in good work well composed, written and spelt. And in
the field of mathematics, some of the pupils have been grasping
ideas which one usually finds only in the secondary school,
whilst even amongst the less able children, "maths" have
acquired meaning and reached a standard in no way inferior to
that in the formal school with sum books, table charts and
frequent "tests."

If you are in doubt about the attainments of children in a less
formal type of school, ask what records are kept on each child.
In most infant schools, children's attainments are regularly
recorded, to make sure they have covered the necessary ground —
what reading standard they have reached, for instance, or what
mathematical concepts they have grasped, at age five, six or
seven. This means that even without "tests" at this stage, the
teacher knows exactly how far John or Jane has come on during
each year, even though no report may have been issued to the
parent. In other freely directed schools, each child may have a
little book in which he himself records his work for the week —
what reading book he has gone on to, what mathematical

"games" he has been playing, what he has written about or "found out." The staff, by looking through these books, keep a check on each pupil's progress, and any parent, therefore, can tell how a child is getting on, even though he may only appear to be "playing" at school. If you feel uneasy because you hear so much from your five or six year old about bricks and building, "playing" at shops or hospitals, or other games, and not enough about books or sums, you could have a chat with his teacher and discuss the records together.

Whatever type of school your child attends at five, you should be sure that he is going to be handled with gentleness, not over-awed or over-punished. This is not likely to happen in a freer school, but there are still, unhappily, too many formal schools where "discipline" is the keyword to class order, and where children go in actual fear of some teacher and what she may do to them if work is not up to standard or behaviour not perfect. It seems a shameful thing, today, to find five year olds heavily punished, sometimes with the cane or strap, in spite of the fact that it has been made abundantly clear by the Department of Education and Science that physical punishment is not accept-able, and should be on the way out, particularly in infant schools. Some local authorities actually forbid it for infants (for example, Wiltshire), so that a parent whose child is being persistently smacked or caned at school should see the head teacher and refer to the local authority's handbook. There is also an association — the Society of Teachers Opposed to Physical Punishment, or STOPP — with a parents' group which you could join. And of course such a matter would be suitable for raising at a meeting of the school parent—teacher association, if there is one.

One final point about choice of a free or formal school lies in this idea of a parent—teacher organization, or its equivalent in friendly relations between parents and staff. Not all good schools have actual parent—teacher associations, though there is a National Federation of P.T.A.s which will give advice about how to set about founding one, if you want to do so. But there are many others who, without any formal organization, still manage to make parents feel that it is "their" school and that they are welcome to a share in their children's education.

It is easy to find out, either by direct question or by talking to other families, whether there is some degree of participation between home and school. It is worth making a real effort to enter your child's name at one which does regard parents as important, and able to contribute, in one way or another, to the good of the school and the happiness and security of the children in it.

Village schools

You may live in a rural district, and be wondering whether to enrol your child at the local village school or to look further afield, even if it involves travelling. What are the pros and cons of a small village school? Space, certainly, may be cramped, lighting or heating or sanitary facilities may be inadequate, playgrounds may be dull affairs with little provision for "adventure" play on a creative scale. There may be only two or three staff (nearly all one-teacher schools have disappeared, though here and there they exist for infants only, whilst juniors travel to a bigger school in another district).

On the other hand, many village primaries offer advantages which, though not always apparent as you pass the school in the village street, can be very real. Go inside, and it is probable that you will find walls painted in gay colours, small washbasins and toilets installed along a corridor, partitions taken down and window sills lowered to make the whole building more light and airy. One which I visited in a very remote village looked un- promising from the exterior, but as soon as I opened the door it was a blaze of colour, with paintings done by the children and hung along the walls, "bays" devoted to different activities with bright, attractive models and materials, a nature corner full of flowers, and the old, dull passage which used to divide "Infants" from "Juniors" painted white and used as an "art gallery" for pupils' work, both in painting and in craft. The porch had been transformed into a carpentry corner where the boys could hammer freely without disturbing the others. This was a tiny village school which a parent might easily have turned down in favour of the new primary in the nearby town. Yet the education here was quite as good, and there were the other advantages of accessibility (daily travelling is very tiring for a five year old) and the friendly "family" feeling which only a small school can engender.

Indeed, it is this family feeling which often makes a village primary a good choice, where the head is progressive. Classes will be smaller, and the large age range may have advantages in keeping brothers and sisters together and encouraging individual or small group work. In addition, a village teacher who lives in the neighbourhood knows the parents and the district, and can draw on the resources of both. Out of school visits to farms, castles, the blacksmith's shop, are much easier in the country, on a small scale. Local craftsmen and others may have much to give, fathers can be enlisted, sometimes, to come and talk to the children about their work, or mothers to help the teacher take a group of children to the local pond to observe the life of water creatures and plants there. Advantage, too, can be taken of the weather, or the seasons, where the school is small enough to allow everybody to "down tools" on a sunny day and go out.

Staffing is sometimes difficult in a village school, but some counties are making up for this by providing visiting teachers with specialist talents — say, in music, or drama, or helping backward learners with remedial teaching — and some, like Oxfordshire, are trying to link village schools with each other by providing a shared minibus which can take parties from several small schools on visits and expeditions which would normally not be possible due to staff shortage. Shared activities like music festivals or sports meetings can also link rural schools together and widen their horizons, as well as providing more facilities for team games and the chance of meeting other pupils with parallel interests.

So just because your little village school seems a small affair, and has a slightly old fashioned air, do not take it for granted that the education there is inferior. It may well be better for your child than being a "country" pupil at a "town" school, besides saving all the wear and tear of travel.

Independent schools

You may, of course, decide to send your child from the first to a fee-paying school. If you are opting out of the State system, this needs to be done with considerable thought. A child headed for the public school sector will almost certainly require private school education along "prep school" lines from about the age of nine, and will have to have his name put down many years ahead at the public school of your choice. There are few State schools which can provide the combination of subjects and specialized teaching which would get a child through Common Entrance to a public school at thirteen, even though it is technically possible to switch from State to public school system from the ordinary secondary school. A good prep school knows just what is needed, and also usually has the contacts which help to get pupils into the most suitable public school; often there are traditional links between prep and public schools, of which a parent will be aware.

Many parents start their children at the local primary, and transfer them to prep or private schools at around eight or nine. But here again, it is necessary to think and plan ahead, for not every prep or private school is able to take children at short notice.

There are also other considerations for a parent who is giving thought to private education of any kind, not only "public school" but any type of independent schooling. (It must be only England that refers to the private schools as "public" — something which often confuses foreigners!) Fees mount steadily; while they may be easily within your reach for one child just beginning his education, it soon becomes a different matter when there are several children to be privately educated, and the fees are doubled by the time a pupil is ten and trebled at fifteen. Moreover, there are other expenses — travel, pocket money, parents' visits, uniform — besides the tuition and/or boarding fees. Educational insurance can help to spread the load, and there are also bursaries and scholarships available. Some of these, such as scholarships for the sons of professional men like doctors or clergymen, or for children born in a special area, are not always widely known, and it is worth consulting the reference section of your public library for information about financial help obtainable. But any family contemplating private education must go thoroughly into all the expenses involved, before important decisions are made.

Many parents prefer independent schooling for their children because they have ideas of their own about how they want their sons or daughters educated. Certain religious bodies, such as the Roman Catholics, the Quakers, and the Methodists, have their

own schools, some of which may have junior departments taking
quite young children. Parents may also want very progressive
education which is only provided in some half-dozen particular
private schools. It is important to make sure that any private
school you choose is "recognized," which means that certain
minimum standards of building, staffing and teaching are met,
and it seems likely that very soon there will be no more unrecognized schools allowed by the State. It is also becoming
increasingly common to find private schools linking with the
State system in many ways; offering places to pupils from State
schools at thirteen or eleven; joining forces with neighbouring
State schools in certain activities, such as musical or dramatic
festivals; or even, as one famous progressive "independent"
school in Devonshire is now doing, allying with a comprehensive
school in the neighbouring town to share resources, and even
opening a nursery school with places for fee-paying and non-fee-
paying under fives drawn from its own junior department and
from the local village. As the two types of school, State and
independent, draw closer together in the future, you may find
in your own district growing possibilities for obtaining the best
of both types for your child. But until the stage of full
integration comes, if you want your child to be privately
educated, the time to consider it is not at thirteen, or even nine
or ten, but right now at the beginning of his school career.

What should you look for in choosing a private school for a
five year old? The views of other parents are always most useful,
though you should bear in mind that your own five year old may
have different needs from those of the one next door who is so
happy at the private school round the corner. Some parents put
great emphasis on good speech and good manners, others on
academic education which will "get a child on," others value
small classes above all else, even if the teaching is rather formal.
Private schools may have classes of from twelve children
upwards, which compares favourably with the average thirty to
forty of the State infant schools. Ask about the staffing, judging
not only from the prospectus (which often lists visiting or part-
time teachers alongside regular ones, or fails to mention un-
qualified "helpers" or students) but from direct enquiry of the
head teacher.

Visit the school, if possible, while the children are there, and with the aim of finding out definite points about the private school. Are the children well mannered and willing to direct and help you? Are the class-rooms filled with desks, or is there play space and room for "activities"? Does the teacher in the room do all the talking, or do the children participate? Is there sufficient outdoor space for "adventure" play for the youngest ones, as well as for team games for older pupils?

At a State school, too, you do know in general (or you can find out) what methods are in use and what approaches are recommended for teaching. State teachers go on courses, read circulars, and have the support of County "advisers" who are specialists in certain subjects. In a private school, none of this may be true; your child will be educated along the lines which the Head approves, or according to the policy of a board of governors. This situation should be watched, for it is important to know, not only how your child is being taught, but what effect the particular type of teaching, and discipline, is having on him. And only you can tell that.

What will happen on entry?

What will happen to your child when the school doors close on him for the first time and he has to manage without you? Is there anything you can do to help him bridge this terrific gap — for that is how it feels to a five year old — between family and class-room? Most head teachers encourage parents to bring children to school on a casual visit during the term before entry. They want to know some particulars — name and age of child, and address, for instance — and they also like children to feel familiar with the school surroundings before they actually start. Mother may be able to show a child where to hang his coat on the first day, where he will wash his hands and go to the lavatory (particularly important for a nervous five year old) and perhaps where he will find himself on that first morning, what toys he will play with, and what books are in the "library" corner or dolls in the Wendy house. All this helps a child to feel less timid when beginning school, and can serve as a useful talking point during the weeks preceding school entry.

Some head teachers, as in certain areas of Hampshire, have a special method of entry, whereby groups of children about to

start school (usually the term after their fifth birthday) are invited to come along before the actual date, to meet each other and
their teacher. Mothers are encouraged to stay and play a part in
helping teacher and child to get to know each other. The
children are treated just as they are at home, allowed to pick up
toys and play with them, handle class-room material, and ask
questions. Other schools adopt "staggered" entry, whereby
some newcomers arrive on the first day, and, when they are
settled in, others follow them a few days later, and perhaps a
further group comes the following week. This enables the teacher
to get her pupils settled more gradually.

Other districts (parts of Gloucestershire, for example) send
families of new entrants a questionnaire, called in some schools
"Introduction to My Child." The mother is asked to answer a
number of questions (by marking the reply with a tick) so that
the future teacher can learn something about the child in her
care. "Does your child fight or cry when he doesn't get his own
way?" might be one question. "Can he go to the lavatory by himse
"Can he fit things together, such as puzzles?" "Does he enjoy
using pencils and crayons, dough, clay and paint?" "Has he been
to play group or nursery school?" Parents answer such questions
with "usually," "seldom," "occasionally" or "often," thus
building up a general picture of their child to help the teacher
when he arrives in her class.

One primary head teacher whom I know has her own method
of "making friends" with future pupils. She sends a personal
letter to each child telling him she is looking forward to meeting
him, welcoming him to the school, and describing a little of what
goes on there. Five year olds coming to this school feel very
important people when they receive their own special "letter,"
and school entry is looked upon as an exciting new experience.
Another head sends a similar letter to both father and mother
of each new pupil, inviting them to look round the school
before their child begins, and asking for some background
details.

If the school makes no attempt at "introduction," then you
can at least invite some children who already go there to come
along to tea, and bring a book or a drawing or a model with
them, to show your own child and awaken his interest. Getting
an older child to come with you both on the first day is often a

good way of avoiding last minute panic and tears; it usually
relieves at least some of the inevitable tension. If you are not
allowed to go in with your child and settle him down with a toy,
or to play with another pupil he knows, it will help if you make
your goodbye as brief as possible, promising that you will be
back at the playground gate at a stated time to fetch him home.
There may be tears, especially if he has not been to play group
or nursery school before, but a hug and a cheery wave of the
hand do a lot to help, and something brought from home (a
picture post card to show the teacher, or a favourite model car
tucked into a pocket) often eases the way in to the new
surroundings.

Infant schools have different ways of introducing their
children into the group. Where "family grouping" is followed,
there will already be older ones fully settled in and able to keep
a friendly eye on newcomers. Children are often very good at
this. But where the reception class consists of some thirty to
forty children, all new together, things may be difficult.

Even here, however, a good teacher will find ways and means.
I watched one young reception class teacher gathering up her
flock of rather tearful newcomers from the entrance hall where
their mothers had just left them. "Who's coming to play puffer
trains?" she called; and in a minute, the motley crowd of
youngsters had turned itself into a long line of children, hands on
each others' shoulders, gaily puffing down the corridor into
their new class-room. Tears were rapidly drying as they realized
that at any rate, the first step into school was a game they could
enjoy.

What will be the routine for your child's first morning?
Probably he will be found an occupation, playing with the dolls'
house, or doing a puzzle, while the teacher sorts out her flock,
taking down details about morning milk and dinner money, and
whether and when each one will be met by mother at the end of
the day.

In the playground, which may seem rather big and noisy to a
timid youngster, and at dinner time if he stays to a midday meal,
there will probably be someone to "mother" him — if not a
teacher, then an older infant, or one from the Juniors, or a
friendly grown-up "school aide" or "dinner lady" whose job it is
to help the teacher with supervision. Often it is a good idea to

let a five year old come home to dinner, if at all possible, for the first week or two. Time at home, however brief, helps to break up a long day and reassures him that the family is still there. On the other hand, most children nowadays enjoy staying to dinner, not always because they have to, but simply because they like eating with their friends and have more chance to play. This, however, sometimes takes time, and rather than force school dinner on a reluctant five year old, it is better to have him home, and wait for the day when he suddenly decides that he'd like to stay "to be with my friends."

What are school dinners like? Few mothers realize what a lot of organization goes into the preparation of school meals, but if you were to visit County Hall and talk to the school meals organizer, you would find a very well planned system, with a staff responsible for catering, buying, preparing, cooking and serving food at all levels, and a scientifically balanced menu. Today more than half of all school children stay to dinner, so the whole business has to be properly run, and counties have their training schemes to ensure that the ordering and cooking of food is never left to chance.

In many infant schools there is some choice of menu, and children are rarely forced to eat what they dislike (if they are, there is something wrong). They may, however, be encouraged to "try" new foods, or to take just a little, even if less than a normal portion. Some have cafeteria meals, where children serve themselves with as much, or as little, as they want. Others have "family service," where children sit in groups of seven or eight at a table, and an older child, perhaps one of the Juniors, acts as "mother" and serves the food. In other instances, teachers sit with the children, though there is no longer any compulsion on them to do this. The probability is that even if he has been rather a "fussy eater" at home, your child will find a new edge to his appetite once he gets the habit of staying to school meals like the rest.

In rural districts, school dinners may be brought from some central point, and kept hot in special containers, or some children may bring packed lunches. Conditions of meals vary so much from place to place that no two schools are exactly alike in the way they organize dinners, though the content of them is always under the supervision of the school meals organizer.

Where your child constantly brings home complaints, it is as well to check with other mothers before doing anything about it, for children sometimes rather enjoy grumbling, just to gain mother's attention when they come home, even though they may have nothing to grumble at!

In a few schools, the head actually invites mothers occasionally to come and join the school dinner and see for themselves what it is like. This naturally means prior arrangement, but it could be an interesting experience if this is the situation at your child's school.

Dinner break, of course, gives a chance for a five year old to relax a little; but even so, there are some who find the regular school day too long. A recent survey of "exhausted infants" produced cases where children had had to leave home very early to catch the school bus, and did not return until late. (One six year old had to leave at 8.10 in the morning and walk fifteen minutes to the school bus stop; and in the evening, though her class ended between a quarter and half past three, she still had to wait until 3.55 for the bus home, which collected senior children at 4; she finally reached home at 4.45.) This state of things is far too tiring for even an average child, and for a not very robust one it is impossible, even where a school provides day beds for younger ones to rest on in the afternoons. Yet most just have to take their chance along with the others, because mothers do not know how to avoid such a situation. One teacher asked a miserable youngster during morning break, "Have you just started school?" "Oh no," came the heartfelt answer. "I've been here ever since nine o'clock!"

Even though regulations insist that children in State schools must attend both morning and afternoon sessions (private schools, it appears, can offer a shorter day because of a certain lack of definition in the phrase "full-time education"), your doctor can intervene if he thinks the long day is causing undue stress. The loophole in the present law is the phrase "unless exceptional circumstances make this (i.e. full-time attendance) undesirable," which means that you could at least apply for a doctor's certificate that half-day schooling is best for your child. However, there are signs that opinion is moving towards a more flexible school day for infants, especially during their first few weeks.

Most parents find that it helps if their tired five year olds are settled down quietly with a picture book or favourite toy on their return from school, or even put to rest on their beds, before being pestered with questions about "What did you do today?" Few children at this stage could tell you, anyway, exactly what they did do at school; the whole thing is so bewildering, so new and exciting and varied, that they have not the words to describe everything. Sometimes, too, they do not want to talk overmuch about school; it is their own special place, just as father's place of business is to him, and it may be a special thrill to keep it to themselves for a little while. News will soon leak out as novelty wears off.

But if we are content to wait, we shall soon find that most small children enjoy their first experiences at school. If they do not, then there is something very wrong. Naturally there will be grumbles: "Somebody hit me." "They threw my new cap over the wall." "I don't like Jane; she always wants to play skipping, and I don't like skipping." "Why must I take my dress off for P.T.? Do I have to?"

By and large, these minor difficulties can be explained away, or overcome. But if you are satisfied that the general aims of your child's first school are right, and that most of the staff, anyway, are on the side of the child, then you and your youngster can look forward to a happy time ahead.

Abstract art? It's fun for David at his playgroup
where a real easel is available

4

Some parents' questions answered

The primary school to which your child is going will probably be somewhat different from the one you attended at the age of five. Just as the settling-in process is different, with more co-operation with the family and a "first" class-room not very unlike the nursery play-room of the four year old, so the methods and approaches of most primary schools have changed a lot, too. Even if the building happens to be the same, what goes on inside it will probably strike you as very different, and perhaps rather puzzling. In a few cases, parents are really disturbed by what they hear about the local school, usually couched in jargon they cannot understand. What *is* all this about family grouping, streaming and non-streaming, the integrated day and team teaching? What are audio-visual aids and teaching machines? Do they really teach them all about sex — in the primary school? And can parents really play a part in their children's education?

Questions like these nearly always arise during a child's first months at school, and it is as well to be familiar with the terms you will hear, so that you and the teachers both know what is being talked about. Let us start with family grouping, for many infant schools, and not a few junior schools as well, use this method of structuring the teaching that goes on inside those class-room walls.

Family grouping

The method is just what it says — "family" grouping as you would find it in a normal large household. At home, tiny children learn from bigger brothers and sisters, older ones take care of little ones, and the ages have much to give and much to take from each other. Many head teachers today are abandoning rigid age-groups and rearranging their infant schools along "family grouping" lines (sometimes called "vertical grouping") for much the same reasons: they find children learn from each other.

In schools where there is family grouping (i.e. an age range in each class extending over two or more years), teachers often find it is easier to integrate new children into the class. Because only, perhaps, a third of her forty or so charges are "new" at the same time, and there are other, more mature children to help and to suggest new ideas to the younger ones, it is much easier for the teacher to weld newcomers into the group. Just as in the small village school, big children "mother" little ones, showing them where to hang coats, wash hands and so on, and later, perhaps, "hear" them beginning to read, or lend an encouraging hand with model making or painting. From the point of view of the newcomers, too, it is much easier to feel at home when you are with a big brother or sister, or an older friend who already knows the ropes. And it is interesting to watch others reading and writing and playing number games, and to be invited to join in. Vocabulary is extended where younger children learn from their older friends' conversation. And there is less bewilderment, less clamouring for the teacher's attention, when only some of the class are "new."

Older ones benefit, too, from not always being forced to go at the same pace. It helps many children, especially those who like to start slowly, to be able to relapse occasionally into "younger" play, or to repeat their own experiences by guiding a younger child through the first stages of reading or writing. For brighter children, too, being in a group of varying ages and abilities enables them to go at a faster pace; they are not kept back by others, but can find their own level and mature more quickly.

There is another side to this picture, of course. It calls for greater sensitivity on the teacher's part to make sure that each child is really working to potential, and a good deal of expertise in making sure that essential ground is covered — through record-keeping of individual pupils' progress. It also means giving proper attention to the needs of different ages within the group; making time for a story for the tinies, for instance, whilst not neglecting the older ones; choosing music which the younger children can enjoy, whilst extending the musical experience of the more mature older pupils. All this calls for skill and co-operation on the part of the whole of the teaching staff in a family grouped school.

But in another way it is of great benefit to both teacher and child if they can stay together for two or three years, particularly in the infant school. Children develop better within this more stable framework, instead of having to change teachers every year; the teacher, too, gets to know her group, and difficulties can be more easily discussed in the staff-room when all teachers have similar age-ranges to cope with. Many parents seem to like the idea, especially since it allows the teacher to spend more time individually with the slower children whilst the brighter get along at their own pace — often far more quickly than if the age range were all the same. The less able child, too, likes the responsibility of having younger ones around, whom he can help; in a similar age range, he might easily slip into anonymity at the back of the class and be outshone by the more mature pupils. In a mixed aged class, there are always plenty of jobs to go round, for the less academic as well as for the brighter.

One most rewarding moment came for one teacher in a family grouped school when an older child came to her leading a little one, reading-book in hand, and said proudly, "Miss, she can read now!"

The integrated day

When we were at school, the day ran by time-tables, bells sounding every forty minutes or so on a "stop-change" system. Today in many schools parents are surprised to find that the time-table (if it exists at all) is very much more sketchy. Mornings may feature certain periods given over to basic skills — the reading, writing and arithmetic of our youth — but afternoons may be times of free-choice activity. Or perhaps your child's school has no fixed periods, even in the mornings, just blocks of time given over to various things — possibly the same thing for two days on end, or even more, if all the children are busily engaged on some major project.

Where children work in groups, too, you may find several "lessons" going on at the same time, and in family grouped schools the picture may be even more complicated, for children may very well be working not only at different "subjects" but at different levels within these subjects.

The time-tabled approach to lessons has very largely, in many schools, given way to the "integrated day" system, where children's activities are not pigeon-holed into "periods" or kept rigidly separate, but blended together to form a busy whole. This means that there are many groups doing different things, possibly following individual interests, or, again, all contributing towards a common core of interest — something they are all involved in together. In one school I visited recently, a Victorian project was under way. This was a junior school, where the children were just beginning to take an interest in history. All the class were involved in trying to re-create the Victorian scene — how the family lived, what the clothes were like, what the schools did, how fathers earned their living. On the day I was there, groups of children were busy on their project, using books, maps, "Victoriana" brought from home, paints, modelling materials, dressing-up clothes. Lessons had blended together to form one busy day — probably two or three, for the project was an extensive one — and reading, writing, number, history, geography, social studies, art, handwork, drama were all going on together. These children were so absorbed that no end-of-period bell could stop them; indeed, it was quite a job to get them to go home when the end-of-day bell finally sounded.

How different all this seems from the time-tabled approach of our youth! Yet it is based on a carefully observed principle — that a child does his best work when allowed to concentrate on and continue with the job in hand. Children like to get to grips with something that interests them, and a child motivated by such interest does not want to be interrupted just as he is getting down to his job. The old idea of "fragmenting" the day into lessons makes no use of the child's inner drive towards completing the work in hand. So in many schools children are now being encouraged to become wholly involved in the task of the moment.

To a parent it may often look as if the day's work at school is totally unplanned. But the very reverse of this is true. Teachers need to meet constantly to discuss what is being done, and what opportunities are likely to arise, bearing in mind the needs of each group of children and how to further them. But the planning may be done by the staff from day to day, meeting informally and filling in large blocks of activity on a common time-table. One teacher, seeing a growing interest in music in one group, may take over the music room for an afternoon session with the "band," another may be ready to do mathematical work with a group of pupils who are keen, whilst several others may work together helping children with a many-sided project in which a number of them are involved.

Team teaching

This brings us on to another term which often puzzles parents — team teaching. Have the days of the old class teacher gone? In many schools the class teacher is still the main person with whom the child is in touch, but there is a growing movement today to extend responsibility through the school in accordance with the varying interests and skills of *all* the teachers.

A flexible or integrated day means that children will be doing many things at once, and that calls for many skills on the part of the staff. Some schools like to "pool" what resources they find amongst their staff, so that instead of the one-teacher-one-class approach, there is time in the day for the children to benefit in larger groups from the enthusiasm and knowledge of particular teachers.

Music, drama, mathematics may be the strong points of certain staff, and it seems a pity that this special experience should not be deployed to the greatest advantage. With more open school planning — "bays" instead of closed-door class-rooms, and more access between "resources" areas where different materials are kept — it is now possible to gather groups of children together under the supervision of one teacher, or a group of teachers who can share the work, acting more as guides and consultants. This does not mean that your child will suffer through having no one teacher to whom he specially "belongs." Children can have a "home bay" which is theirs, where they meet every day, and perhaps spend the whole morning together with their "home" teacher, scattering during the afternoon to various other bays or class-rooms where a team of teachers, or a music or drama specialist, is ready to supervise group work on some particular topic, and then returning to their own base.

Team teaching enables the staff of a school to work together, using any special abilities they may have for the good of all. It is naturally easier to organize in a school with a fairly open building plan, and a flexible time-table, but as more and more schools fall into this pattern, it looks as though more emphasis may be laid on the "team" aspect of teaching — and usually this approach is enjoyed much more by both pupils and staff. Children get to know, not only one, but all the teachers, and catch something of the specialist's or craftsman's own enthusiasm (many teachers work alongside the children at such crafts as pottery or painting). Teachers, too, know all the children instead of only one group, and still retain their particular interest in their own little "family" when at the end of the day children return to their "home bay" to discuss what they have been doing, finish written work, talk over an experiment, and make plans for tomorrow.

Everything here depends on good liaison between the teachers. Where staff get together at the end of the day to pool their findings, talk about the children and their difficulties, and exchange experiences so that the "home" teacher knows what her children have been learning, then team teaching can prove a really fruitful experience.

Streaming

By streaming is usually meant the division of children into classes, according to ability. In a family grouped school there would be no streaming, for all children would enter and pass through the school as individuals, being taught according to their needs and abilities within a mixed group. In many schools, however, even in the "top infants," and certainly in the juniors, children are graded according to mental ability into A, B or C streams or their equivalents. It is easier in some ways to teach a class of similar ability, and in very large schools with a staff shortage, it is extremely difficult to group children in any other way, for coping with a group of mixed ability needs plenty of time, skill and patience.

But from the child's point of view, it is gradually coming to be recognized that streaming does not help so much as hinder, and there is a gradual but steady trend away from streaming towards mixed-ability grouping. For one thing, rigid streaming at six, seven, eight or nine according to a child's academic attainments narrows his social experience. He mixes only with his own type of child, yet in real life he will not live in A, B or C streams, and he cannot come to understand other people and their problems if he has gone all through his school-days in a stream with children just like himself.

For another thing, it has been frequently and conclusively shown that children tend to behave according to our expect-ations of them. If we dub them "poor material" at an early age, then they are likely to feel themselves "poor material" for the rest of their school lives. Any child in a C stream soon gets to realize that nothing much is expected of him by the teacher. And if his parents expect more of him, he tends to become anxious and nervy. Parents can so easily infect their children with their own anxiety, and most worry if their child is only in a B or C stream, however the name may be disguised. One teacher even tells of seven year olds who come to her to ask, "Mummy says, what letter is this class?" hoping, of course, that it is the A stream.

Streaming depends upon the wishes of the head. Some do not stream at all; others not in the infants or lower juniors, but from nine or so upwards. It is important to find out what your child's school favours, if you have strong feelings for or against streaming; and it may even be possible to get him into a non-streamed school outside the usual zone if parents insist. Teachers, of course, vary in their attitude towards it. Many feel it makes too heavy demands upon them; but on the other hand, many prefer to gain experience of varying types of children and to pool their problems; there can be no question in an unstreamed school of all the bright children being given to Mr X, who therefore has no sympathy or interest in the slower learners, who have always gone to poor Miss Y.

Children, too, can be helped to learn, not only by their teachers, but by each other, and this often happens in the unstreamed school. Difficulties can be explained better by children who themselves have mastered them; a poor vocabulary can be enriched by the larger store of words used by children

from more articulate homes. Naturally, there must be plenty of
materials, and a large supply of books, in the non-streamed
school, and enough visual aids and teaching equipment to
stimulate the slower ones. There must, too, be continual
checking on the attainments of each child to make sure that
no one gets left behind. But given these safeguards, it does seem
as though the schools of tomorrow are going to be largely
unstreamed. Particularly if they are to be freed from the
demands of a selective examination at eleven, there appears
every indication that rigid streaming of the old A, B and C type,
which brought so much anxiety to so many children and
parents, is on the way out, at least in the primary school.

Audio-visual aids

Much is talked today about teaching aids — audio-visual aids in
particular. What are they, and how can they help your child? Can
they ever replace the traditional methods of teaching we ourselves knew — the book and the blackboard, and the personal
relationship of teacher and pupil?

Some parents view even the simplest audio-visual aid as an
easy way out for the teacher: "letting my Mary watch TV," as
one mother put it, "while Miss X gets on with her knitting."
Others regard all mechanical teaching aids with scorn, as a
passing fashion: "talking hardware," as I once heard it
described.

Of course these aids are never meant to replace ordinary
teaching. They are not a soft option for the teacher, who has
to do a lot of preparation before even a TV film is shown, not
to mention the follow-up work afterwards; nor are they merely
"hardware," any more than any other scientifically devised
instruments with a purpose in view. The purpose of these aids is
to help a child learn, in fields which he could never even enter
if confined to the class-room, the blackboard and the book.

First and oldest "aid" is the radio. Broadcasting to schools
has been going on for more than 45 years now, and more than
16,000 primary schools use the programmes, a quarter being
rural schools with only a small staff, where the scope of
teaching can be enormously increased by radio. More recently,

TV has brought out its own educational programmes for all ages. Most schools' programmes last for about 20 to 25 minutes, and are produced to fit into a school's teaching programme for the term or the year. Programmes are kept up to date by the Schools Broadcasting Council, which has special liaison officers to contact the schools, and the content of broadcasts is under continual review to make sure it meets the changing needs of the class-room.

There are primary school radio and TV programmes on a huge variety of subjects, from Music Workshop, Roman Britain, and Primary French to films about animals, suggestions for stories and poems, and, most recently, beginners' reading lessons. Children enjoy them so much that often their greatest punishment is being told "you can't watch the TV lesson today." For smaller schools particularly, they are an enormous fillip to the teaching programme, bringing life before the child's ears and eyes in a way normally impossible in the classroom, and they are so well put over that, far from deadening a child's imagination, they offer endless starting points for experiment and talking points for discussion.

Films and filmstrips are also widely used. They have many advantages, in that they can be ordered in advance, used at times suitable to the school's organization, and watched again and again by different groups. They may be black and white or in colour, and last from 12 minutes to 40 or 45. Teachers find them particularly useful where diagrams or animated pictures are required for class work, and the best of them can be very good indeed. Here again, subjects range from teaching French and junior science to "The Craft of the Potter," "Writing through the Ages," "Rabbits and Hares" and "The Changing Face of Japan."

Many primary schools use tape recorders, which are very easily adapted to children's needs particularly in the fields of drama, music and speech. They are also a great help for revision work, for assisting a child to "catch up" after absence, or for remedial teaching for slower learners. The tape recorder can record an individual child's "talk" on a chosen subject, take down a class play, act as a check on a French accent, or inspire a class to writing through hearing a great piece of literature or a moving poem. And it is portable — a great advantage, as this means that schools can even exchange tapes between themselves — a town school with a country one, or even an English school with one abroad.

In some schools children learn to use a tape recorder themselves. One group of city children in a very impoverished district used a "tape" to interview people — shoppers in the market, for example; to take to the Zoo to record animal noises which could be incorporated in a "Zoo" book later; and to stimulate and record discussions. The tape recorder here did a great deal to get children talking and concentrating, and proved an invaluable aid to learning.

The same school also used film loops and slide projectors, the children making their own slides. Some American visitors to the school, seeing the enthusiastic use made of all these mechanical teaching aids, presented the head mistress with a polaroid camera, which takes "instant" pictures. This, she says, is so invaluable in her work with the children that she would never be without it.

Perhaps the most controversial of all mechanical aids is that known as the teaching machine. Some parents are horrified at the very idea of a "machine" doing duty for a teacher. In reality this is just a device which sets out a learning programme step by step, to instruct and test the learner at his own pace. It was never intended to replace the teacher, only to supplement teaching by giving children something at which they can work at their own pace, testing themselves as they go along, and increasing concentration and confidence. A child can sit at such a machine and advance steadily through a programmed sequence of "frames" putting questions or challenges. As each is worked through, he can test his answer; where it is wrong, it will be followed by explanation and correction, and where it is right, the child is allowed to go on to the next step.

Teachers are impressed with some of the results they find. Instead of being met with criticism from the teacher or comments from the class when an answer is wrong, the child is corrected quite impersonally in a friendly manner. Juniors at one Midland school, who used to find spelling and vocabulary tests difficult and boring, now work these out on teaching machines quite happily. A chore has become a game with a challenge, says their teacher, and they are now learning new words and spellings at a greatly improved rate.

No one pretends that the use of any aid is going to replace the individual teacher. Personal relationships are vital to education, especially where young children are concerned. But as we advance further into the age of science, we shall readily come to see how much these audio-visual aids can contribute towards children's learning.

Sex education

Not long ago it would have been considered quite unsuitable to introduce sex instruction into a primary school curriculum. Recently, however, many schools have taken advantage of the TV series on this subject, and of film strips, to incorporate sex education into the various other subjects in which a young child is naturally interested; and in others, teachers are ready to talk about sex and birth in a way which would never have been countenanced a generation ago.

In part, this is due to the earlier age at which children, especially girls, are reaching maturity. Nowadays it is not uncommon to find young pupils menstruating before the end of their primary school years. Thus the whole question of when to give sex information has come under review. Children, too, are more ready to discuss these things, and frequently want answers to their questions given in a more comprehensive and scientific way than many families can manage.

Many teachers feel that the experimental year, in which TV and filmstrip sex lessons went out to junior schools for the first time, has been a success. Sex differences, and the normal process of birth, are questions at the back of every young child's mind, whether they are voiced or not; and it is usually teachers and parents, not children, who feel embarrassed at talking about them. Where teachers, however, have been willing to answer children's questions as they crop up, and have "built in" instruction on these subjects as part of the normal process of learning about the body and its growth, the results have usually proved satisfactory.

True, the best introduction to sex for your child is to answer his questions as they arise, in the very early years, when, "Where did I come from?", "How are babies born?" and "Why is John's body different from mine?" are asked purely for inform-ation. A child who has been answered frankly, briefly and simply (a safe rule is never to give answers which may later have to be unlearned) before school age will be well equipped with a basic knowledge of what birth and babies are all about and, even more important, with an unselfconscious attitude towards it all. At primary age, before a child's emotions are engaged, many teachers find it perfectly possible to give the necessary information, at around nine or ten years of age, along with normal teaching on human and animal growth.

If your child's school is likely to do this, you will probably be given a circular inviting you to attend a forum for discussion between parents and teachers. Parents naturally can keep their child away from such lessons, but in fact very few do so. At one school where this teaching was due to take place for the first time, more than 300 parents attended the introductory meeting, and many mothers and fathers told of their relief that "at last" their children would be better informed than they themselves had been at primary age. In this school, film strips were shown in the course of a term's programme about "How your body works," by the class teacher, whom the children already knew and trusted. Questions were answered, and books made available in the book corner — not pushed at the children, but left for them to read if they wanted to. The children accepted the teaching readily, and with very few giggles or blushes; if these did occur, they soon gave way to absorbed interest in what was being discussed, and as soon as the children knew they could talk freely, questions came thick and fast. "I only wish I'd had the whole thing brought out into the open when I was this age," one father commented to the teacher afterwards. "It would have saved me so much worrying. When they get to the secondary school it's usually too late."

There is little doubt that the subject of sex, now it has been introduced into even a few primary schools, will remain and receive even wider recognition. Nevertheless the obligation will still be on us, as parents of young children, to give the first basic information very simply in the early years, so that our child, when the time comes, can join freely in class discussion.

Home and school

One of the vital elements in your child's education at any level will be the amount of co-operation between school and home.

All go-ahead teachers feel that education should ideally be a partnership between parent and teacher. It is certainly not something which starts at 9 a.m. and ends at 4, but goes on all the time, in the home as well as at school; and so it is essential that parents shall have a part in the work of the school, and that teachers shall know the home backgrounds of the pupils they teach.

The importance of this co-operation was recognized by the Plowden Committee which showed in its Report that 80 per cent of primary schools have parent—teacher associations. There is a National Federation of P.T.A.s which can give advice about their formation and support their work, yet many head teachers are far from enthusiastic about them, and many definitely refuse to have one — "We've got an Open Day once a term; what more do you want?"

It is impossible in cases like these to set up a P.T.A. in face of opposition. And all too often, where a P.T.A. does exist it turns out to be just a group of parents raising money for school events — a new radio, a swimming pool — with the same people doing all the work, and a large backlog of parents too uninterested to join. A really active P.T.A. will include most parents — one head master of a primary school in Essex automatically enrols all his parents in the P.T.A. at the same time as he enrols the children, and it will do far more than just money raising. With the co-operation of the staff, a parents' association can play a very active part in school life, not only meeting regularly for talks and discussions, but actually working for the school in a number of practical ways.

What can you do if your child's school does not have a P.T.A.? It takes a great deal of tact to approach a head teacher with a request for one; parents have no legal right to be represented, as they have in many countries such as the U.S.S.R. where every class has its parents' committee, and they do not often use their influence to make themselves felt at school, as occurs frequently in the United States. Many are apologetic about even going to see the head teacher: "How many mums have come to me and said, 'I didn't like to trouble you!' " observed one headmistress.

Sometimes partnership can begin by one parent offering help. After all, a teacher cannot know beforehand what parents have to offer; and occasionally a child's remark ("My dad's the best carpenter in the world!") can lead to a Dad's help being enlisted, through mutual co-operation, to make a slide for the reception class, or provide offcuts of wood for sanding down for building blocks. One very spectacular gift, which did wonders in a school for backward boys, was a parent's offer of an ancient Land Rover, which was towed into the playground and immediately swarmed over by small boys. "I simply can't describe," said one of the teachers here, "what this gift from a parent has meant to these boys. Not only has it sparked off enthusiasm in itself, but that enthusiasm seems to be spreading into school work as well. It's as if at last something has caught their imagination, and I can now find ways of building on that to help them with their lessons in the class-room."

In other cases, partnership is first offered through the school, arising almost by accident. In one village school, the children were allowed the use of a swimming pool on Saturday mornings; but the pool was nine miles away, so parents were asked whether they could provide transport. Not only did they volunteer, but in the end actually helped with the swimming lessons, and some parents even took a life saving course so as to be able to teach this to the pupils.

It was not long before parents found themselves fully involved with the school, not only on Saturdays but during the week. One, who was a potter, offered the loan of a kiln; another father made a thermometer for it; another who was the village blacksmith made some beautiful replicas of Bronze Age axes to illustrate points in the history lessons at the school. When the teachers ran a project on Queen Victoria's reign, nearly every child brought something to school as illustration; and when some Roman remains were unearthed nearby, parents joined children in a "dig." Soon the whole local community had become involved with the school.

In cases like these, sometimes an official P.T.A. is formed and at other times it scarcely seems necessary; co-operation is just taken for granted. There are many ways in which co-operation can take place without any official organization. One primary school I know in North London has a notice in its entrance hall: "Parents and Visitors Welcome," and outside the head's room a chair is always waiting, and a notice on the door says, "Please knock and the head master will see you as soon as possible." Since this is a multi-racial district, notices are written both in English and in Greek, so that Cypriot parents can feel they are just as welcome as British ones.

Another school in Kent sends each family the current issue of the Newsletter, which gives school news and dates of events to which parents are welcome; the booklet carries a special message, "Don't forget — this junior school is your school, and you are welcome at any time. We are always glad to see you, and you may see the way your child works whenever you like."

Parents sometimes actually help in school routine — not as teachers, but as general aides, taking groups of five year olds for sewing, threading needles, helping with cutting out, hearing children read. In one school mothers come with younger children every Wednesday afternoon to make soft toys for the annual bazaar, or aprons for the painting classes, or to bind books or sew costumes for a play. "It prevents a lot of loneliness amongst young mums," says the head mistress here, "and also gives them a useful glimpse into what goes on inside the school. Only two or three of them help in the class-room, but when they do, their assistance can be of the greatest value — we have so many children who want a bit of extra 'mothering'." Fathers too can play a part; one junior school enlists the aid of a Dad on shift work to coach football once a week. Several schools I have visited invite parents, or grandparents, to join in morning assembly once a week, or to take part in the end-of-week hymn singing session on Friday afternoons, bringing babies with them if they like. Such family participation can often do quite as much as, if not more than, an official parent—teacher organization.

Recently, other groups have been formed to keep parents abreast of their children's education. Such is CASE (the Confederation for the Advancement of State Education), which bands parents together in the interests of home—school partnership. And the Advisory Centre for Education at Cambridge acts as a parents' clearing house for ideas about how to help our children get the best out of the education offered at school. Indeed, the Centre has been so concerned over this question of home—school relations that it has formed the Home and School Council, bringing together the three existing parents' organizations, CASE, the PTA's and ACE, to enable parents to speak with one voice where their children's education is at stake. By joining ACE a parent can receive a regular journal with news of current educational trends, and can also have questions answered about his own child's particular problems.

Parents and the head

As yet, few schools provide complete freedom for a parent to come up and see the head at any time. Undoubtedly this is the ideal, for most of us are a trifle nervous of an official "interview" at our child's school, although there may be pressing reasons for seeking it. Some schools offer special Parents' Evenings at which fathers and mothers can ask about their children's progress or discuss difficulties; but it is not easy to talk in detail about your John or Mary when, as one father put it, "I feel Mrs Jones behind me breathing down my neck all the time."

 Most heads will grant an interview if given notice, and in many cases it is better if information about a particular child can be gathered together from teachers before a parent appears on the scene. Sometimes it is essential to gain the school's co-operation; when there is family illness or separation, when a divorce is pending, or there is some special strain, a child's work and behaviour at school is very likely to suffer, and the chance to mention these things in confidence to a sympathetic head will be well worth while. When a child persistently tries to get out of going to school, again there is something deeply wrong. It may be that he gets bullied on his way to or from school, or dislikes a particular teacher (or is disliked in his turn). These are things a head can quite easily look into, and put right by a judicious word to a teacher or a sharp eye on other children's conduct.

Where work is concerned, a parent is often worried. Usually the school report provides some indication of how John or Jane is getting on, but such reports vary enormously between school and school. Some merely give marks or positions in form, with cryptic comments such as, "Could do better." These should never be taken just at surface value — marks and positions can be very misleading and admit of wide variations, and the "could do better" might easily apply to the teacher, not the child: many a pupil has become bored and apathetic because he is being badly taught.

A few schools are taking the whole business of school reports
much more seriously, and really trying to put across a picture of
the child at school. One head I know issues a three-page report;
the first page is devoted to "How we see your child," the second
is a subject report, and the third a page for parents to add
comments of their own. If you can obtain this kind of picture
about your child's performance, and know that the teacher in
turn understands your side of it, then there will be much less
need to worry about John's progress or go to the school to
talk things over.

Where you are worried, however, over gradual deterioration
in work, or a child's obvious inability to cope, then most Heads
will welcome a chance to discuss the problem. Sometimes a
parent's own expectations are too high. In other cases, some
small adaptation of home conditions — giving John a quiet
corner in which to practise writing, or do extra reading, at
home — is all that is needed for him to catch up. Where you find
other parents, too, are worried or puzzled about their children's
progress, or the methods being used to teach them, it is sometimes worth while suggesting to a Head that you would all
appreciate a Parents' Evening, when the new i.t.a., or the new
maths methods, or the new system of family grouping, can be
explained.

Happily, today, there is every sign that, however slowly, home
and school are coming closer together, and co-operating for the
good of the child. A recent enquiry showed that some 28 per
cent of the variation in primary children's school performance
could be attributed, not to "good" homes or "good" schools
but simply to parental attitudes — whether or not the family is
seriously involved in education. The Plowden Committee thought
this subject so important that it devoted a whole chapter to the
subject of parental co-operation. So it is worth all the time and
energy parents can spare to make sure that there is a real and
active liaison between home and school, and a real understanding of what modern education is all about.

5
"Maths is all around you"

A primary head teacher tells of an eight year old who was kept away from school one day with a shocking cold. Next morning, when her mother came to explain her absence, she told the teacher of the "terrible time" she had had when her daughter had to be kept at home.

"She cried and cried," said the mother, "when I wouldn't let her come to school. You see, she wanted to do her maths!"

This little girl was at a school where "maths," taught enthusiastically and sensibly by staff who had studied the way children learn, was an integral part of an exciting day. She didn't want to miss it. Yet, more likely than not, when you and I were at school, a child would cry because she didn't want to do her maths, or arithmetic, or sums, as it was called then. To many parents, maths was a subject you got right or wrong, with ticks and crosses in your sum book. It belonged in books, was taught out of books, and was recorded in books. It certainly wasn't, as one small boy in a modern primary school put it, "all around you." And it certainly wasn't fun.

Many people today are still scared of maths because it is, to them, a matter of "getting it right" or "getting it wrong." Or perhaps they are not now scared, because they managed to learn the parrot-like tricks of "getting it right" — to please the teacher, or to pass an exam.

Today, however, there are signs that an entirely new approach is being made to maths, particularly in our primary schools. Go into an infant class in a modern primary school, and you will find a very different attitude to maths from that of a generation, or even a decade, ago. Few children now sit learning tables or doing endless sum cards. Not that tables or sum cards are completely discarded; they may be useful aids to learning. But it is the basic learning that is done so differently.

Today's modern teachers are concerned, not at first with what is learnt in the mathematical field, but how it is learnt: what number is all about. It is the ideas behind number that matter. That is why we see so many small children in infant classes playing — just as they did at nursery school — with bricks and sand and water, conducting a class-room "shop" or a jumble sale with clothes from the dressing-up box, or starting a post office at Christmas time to send out letters to each other. Parents sometimes complain that their children, at this stage, "don't do sums any more," and think there is something wrong. Actually, it is something right — much more right than the conventional sum books, with their ticks and crosses, that we used to bring home from our arithmetic lessons in the infant school.

Approaching maths like this is "right" because it means that before he is concerned with mathematical symbols, a child is becoming familiar with the purpose of number; he is finding what it is all about. If he has attended nursery school, he will take less time to work through this stage, for he will already have discovered weighing and measuring, compared the contents of differently sized buckets or bottles, counted out plates and spoons at dinner time, and found out what is meant by "big," "bigger" and "biggest." You too may have shown him quite a lot of this at home. But when they first begin maths at infant school, most children have to pass through this phase before they concern themselves with number symbols or attempt to work out problems for themselves. They must know *why* we learn maths. And this will provide the stimulus for learning how we record our mathematical discoveries.

New maths

But this is just the play-way to mathematical learning, which we have had with us for a long time. What is even more exciting, to thoughtful parents today, is the "new maths" teaching which is going on in the really forward-looking schools — which, it would not be an over-statement to say, is shaping a revolution in this sphere. I have been in primary schools where young children, just arrived in the class-room, were using, quite unconsciously, a mathematical vocabulary — perimeter, rhombus, diagonal — previously confined to the secondary school: something which no parent or teacher would have expected of them years ago.

And these children were not using such terms parrot fashion; they knew what they were talking about. Children learning this "new maths" are able to advance happily at a surprising pace into the complicated world of mathematics, and, what is more important, to understand the basic concepts of calculation. They have been making discoveries which need mathematical concepts and skills to work out, and so they know what they are doing. This is why maths in such schools is no longer a bugbear, no longer something to get "right" or "wrong," but something to be enjoyed just as the little girl who was kept away from school enjoyed it. To many children, as to her, the missing of a "maths" period can be a real disappointment.

Why and how has this revolution come about? To understand it, we need first to realize what a different place modern mathematics takes today from that of past times. In this space-age world of computers and other machines, there is no more room for the Victorian clerk who used to sit on his stool meticulously keeping his ledgers, and for whom the old type of arithmetic was indispensable. Today a mathematician can practically do without the drudgery of "figures." What he needs to understand is concepts. And what he needs to develop is a flexible mind which can solve the new mathematical problems which are daily occurring as science moves — at an amazing rate — forward into the future.

The fields in which your five year old may find himself working in the future will probably be different from any we can dream of. The problems he will have to solve will be changing all the time. He will need, naturally, to learn the basic skills of maths, but, more important, he will need to assess situations, formulate problems and test out new answers to them. The type of maths teaching he should be having now is the type which will give him clear understanding of basic concepts so that he can enjoy making his own discoveries and finding out answers to his problems. It will be the child who will ask the questions, and the teacher who answers them — or rather, suggests avenues of exploration and encourages discussion.

But there is another factor, too, which has had a bearing on the modern methods of teaching maths to young children. This is the valuable work of the psychologist Jean Piaget of Geneva, whose methods are known to every teacher. Piaget's purpose was to try to understand the way a young child's mind works and the stages he goes through in his learning. He devised a number of play situations for small children, and gave his co-workers clear instructions for dealing with children's responses to them. Through watching and noting, observers were able to perceive what makes a young child's mind "tick" — or, as Piaget himself put it ,what are his mental structures.

Piaget showed us that a child has to pass through certain stages in his journey towards logical thinking, which is what maths is all about. First, his thinking is entirely intuitive. To a four or five year old, things are what they seem: a heap of pebbles may be five, or seven, or ten; "numbers" are just names to him. A tall slim vase of water appears to hold, by its very size, more than a tubby little container — even though they both may in fact hold the same quantity. When he starts school, a child is usually still at this intuitive stage. It takes experience for him to reach the second stage, called by Piaget the stage of concrete operations, when through entering into many different experiences and playing with many kinds of concrete objects, he comes to understand what number really means — that however he arranges his heap of five pebbles, there will always be just five of them (what somebody once called "the fiveness of five"), or that the same amount of liquid poured into differently shaped containers still remains the same. Passing from the first to the second stage of thinking usually takes some two years — the vital years between five and seven, when he is beginning maths at school. From this point on, it will probably take him the rest of his primary school years to discard, gradually, the actual materials with which he works and attain the ability for abstract mathematical thought; though some children, it is true, reach this stage before they get to the secondary school.

A new impetus has been given to maths teaching in today's primary schools as teachers become more familiar with these ideas. They have had very far-reaching effects. Maths has ceased to be an affair of ticks and crosses, or even of answering questions set by the teacher, either in a book, or on the blackboard. The demands which the future will make of our children, for asking questions which are, as it were, "open-ended," call for a new approach, flexible enough to give a child command over situations still to come. Today's maths teacher, even in the primary school, is trying to keep mathematical questions as "open" as possible, encouraging children to explore, handle, ask, "What happens if . . . ?" and to learn the correct vocabulary from the start, to enable them to express their findings accurately. It is surprising, perhaps, when John, barely seven, uses terms which his father recognizes as belonging to the computer age. But why not, if he understands them? This is the language he will have to use in the future.

Much work has been done in this sphere by the Nuffield Foundation, an educational body set up in 1964, which originated the first New Maths project for children between 5 and 13, with the support of the Schools Council and of many local education authorities, and much help from interested teachers. Your child's teacher may well be using the Nuffield "guides," a series of booklets stressing, not *what* to teach, but *how* to learn. These guides have helped many a teacher to realize that children must achieve understanding in maths from the first, instead of learning off mysterious "drills" or reciting tables. The new approach has been discussed at many of the new Teachers' Centres all over the country, and teachers in training are being introduced to Nuffield methods, as well as to some of the new apparatus which is helping young children to learn through experience. Schools today realize the fact that children need to *handle* things — from conkers and beads to milk bottles and sand — for a long time, before they are encouraged to experiment, discuss and finally record. They also realize, increasingly, that this kind of maths cannot be confined to so many set periods a week, or so many minutes per period. John, engrossed in measuring the heights of children in his group, won't want to stop when the bell goes. Indeed, if he is made to do so, his whole enthusiasm may be lost, and he won't bother to go on and record his discoveries in pictorial, graph or written form.

This is why maths today tends to spill over into many sides of school life. John may spend an entire morning measuring and recording, or several days with a bunch of children finding out, as one group did, the effect of wind on balloons, or working out measurements and drawing up plans for making a wooden playhouse in the school yard.

Parents still tend to rate mathematical ability particularly high, especially the sort of ability which can be assessed by a page of tidy sums ticked or adorned with a "star." This is quite natural, for where streaming is the rule, children are very often allotted to the A, B or C streams mainly on mathematical ability, and where exams have to be passed by a certain age, the "markable" type of sum still figures very largely on the exam paper. So it is not surprising if a family is worried because Susan doesn't seem to be bringing home any correctly marked "sum papers," or Alan spends much of his school time running a toy car up and down a slope. Both Susan and Alan may be doing maths in the new way, making discoveries about all kinds of things (even the rate at which different toy cars run down slopes) which are not immediately recorded and may never, even then, be decorated with a tick or a star. Many schools hold special "parents' evenings" at which the new approach to maths is explained, or where parents themselves may even "go back to school" and use the same mathematical materials as their children, making the same discoveries. But if your child's school does not do this, you can still check on whether he is being properly taught in the sphere of maths. For he will be asking questions about the time on the clock, or the distance between two neighbouring towns; he will be collecting data about the family's heights, or sizes in shoes, or the money spent on the weekly grocery order; or he will be taking an intelligent interest in the speedometer readings on the car. These are all meaningful mathematical situations, with answers which it is fun to find out, quite apart from school hours.

There are several other "new maths" schemes beside the Nuffield one, but what they all have in common is the idea of maths as something live and creative, based on concepts which a child can understand and which are suited to the age we live in and the jobs our children will take in the future. Many schools which have not yet gone over completely to any of these systems are nevertheless adapting traditional methods to suit present day attitudes. Often, new ideas grow alongside the old. Some teachers will allow one group of children each day to do "mathematical discovery" work while the others work at "number" in the usual way. Or there may be a "maths table" in a corner of the class-room or the hall, where attractive things are set out to provoke discussion: a ruler or a tape-measure ("What's it for?"), a box of brightly coloured plastic shapes

("What are they called?"), beads for sorting ("Let's put all the red ones together, and then do it another way and put all the big ones together, or all the round ones") or, as I saw in one tiny village school I visited, a set of ancient pewter beer mugs which the teacher had found at the old village inn, ranging in size from biggest to smallest and ornamenting one wall of the room. All these display features will suggest things for groups of children to do, and spark off experiment and discussion which the teacher can use in her daily work with the class.

One school I know uses Friday afternoons, when there is a relaxed atmosphere about the place, as a starting point for introducing a mathematical problem or experiment to which children can work out an answer over the weekend. Here parents can be a great help. If your child comes home from school wanting to make a "plan" of the house, or tells you he has been asked to collect all the mathematical material possible from the Sunday trip in the car, take his request seriously. It is part of a well thought out plan to set mathematical puzzles for children to solve at home.

Mathematical language

One thing your child will be learning at school (and which he may have begun already to learn at nursery school or play group on a limited scale) is to use mathematical language: to talk about numbers, shapes, weights and measures, in the right terms. At home he will already have learnt to distinguish between "big" and "small," "taller than" and "shorter than," though he probably will still have been at the intuitive stage when a pile of counters or bricks is just "a lot" to him, not a definite number, and will have needed your help to count out "two" or "three" or "seven." But all the time he has been unpacking your shopping basket, fitting things together, pouring out and filling, helping with cooking, laying the table, and he will know that words are used for all these experiences, even though they are not yet all meaningful to him.

At infant school, if he is taught on the new lines, he will begin to learn the right words for his experiences. In one class-room a group of fives and some six year olds were playing with various objects, sorting them into labelled groups. They took these objects put each into a round hoop which the teacher had placed on the floor, round ones in this hoop, square ones in that hoop, cylindrical ones somewhere else. At the same time as they were learning to distinguish between different shapes, they were also learning the right names for the shapes. The objects were ordinary ones: Toblerone chocolate boxes (triangular prisms), shoe boxes (rectangular solids), egg boxes (irregular shapes), and others. One little girl picked up a cylindrical detergent container that another child had sorted into the "rectangular solids" hoop. "That doesn't belong here," she said, "It's a cylinder," and promptly put it into the place where it did belong.

Sorting is important, not only because it provides the right names for shapes as a child handles them, but because it gives him the idea of a "set." This is vital to present day mathematics, because the "set" (a collection of things) is an idea which lies at the back of all number experience, and by understanding what a set is you can give yourself a basic tool for all modern technology.

Susan's teacher will point, perhaps, to all the blue things in the class-room. Jane's dress is blue, John's socks are blue, dress and socks are the "same" colour. Marion will draw a "set" of all the things she found on the beach on her seaside holiday: shells, a jellyfish, seaweed, rocks, a baby crab. Later, she will draw a picture of, or write down, another "set" of things that belong together. Gary, six, drew a picture of the model rocket he was making, and wrote down, with sketches, all the things he needed: a wooden round pole, a brass ring, a stick, a square box with a hole in it, a glass pot upside down. By this time, Gary was well able not only to sort out things that belonged to a set, but to write them down and draw them to form a whole. Children now will begin to understand the meaning of "sub-sets": things that float and things that sink, children who go home to dinner and children who stay at school; and will be making charts to record them. They will also be finding out about the order of numbers: Jane and Tom, queuing up for dinner, are "in front of" Mary and Jean, but "behind" Robert and Diane; Mark, drawing a "family" picture of people at home, ranging from tiny baby up to big Daddy, is putting the members of the household in order of size.

Recording these discoveries can be fun. Your child may make

a graph showing children's heights or birthdays in his class, play
a game with the number ladder where pipe cleaner "men"
climb up as you throw a dice, or use number strips of wood or
card, or number spaces chalked on the playground for children
to jump along.

Number relationships are often learned, not by chanting or
memorizing in the old way, or even by using the time-honoured
"plus" and "minus" signs at first, but by discovery methods.
The "plus" sums are sometimes introduced by the "arrow"
symbol. The use of an arrow seems to a small child more sensible
than the use of the plus sign; it is meaningful ("an arrow tells
you where to go") and serves as a transition between using words
and using the symbols of mathematics. It is also an introduction
to the "mapping" which he will learn, later, at secondary level;
when John starts with the numbers 2 and 4 and adds them, and
shows the results, 6, by means of an arrow, his father may
recognize this as the language, more or less, of the computer. To
John, the arrow means "belongs to"; just as it would be sensible
for him to portray an everyday relationship such as "a ball
belonging to John" by drawing a picture of the ball, with an
arrow leading to John, so it is sensible for him to make 2 and 4
belong to 6 by means of an arrow.

Subtraction, that bane of our youth, also becomes meaningful when it is seen not as a "sum" but as a relationship which
makes sense. A bag of counters sorted into pairs should make up
ten. Are there any pairs missing? It will be fun to find out what
makes up ten. Subtraction — the dreaded old "minus" or "take
away" sums — will become a matter of charting the difference
between, say, the number of children who come by bus to
school, and the number who walk; it is seen that more come by
bus, so the children "count on" from the bussers to the walkers,
till the whole class is included. Nobody has talked about
"subtraction," but the children have grasped the "difference."

Later, when it comes to multiplication, the old chanting of
tables is fast giving way to preliminary exploration which leads a
child on to "see" a number relationship rather than parrot it off
by heart. Patty tins for baking come in useful here, and many
infant class-rooms have a baking corner with a real cooker in it.
Jane sees that the patty tins come in more or less standard
sizes: tins with three rows of two, which is the same as two rows

of three; or three rows of four, or four rows of three. In one school, children discovered that five wooden spills could be matched against one garden cane, and there they were, working multiplication to a number base of five. Small boys like putting toy soldiers in lines; four columns of three become, when looked at another way, three columns of four. All this might look like play to the unpractised eye — just Johnny playing at soldiers again, or Jane doing baking; why don't they make them do any work? Actually both Johnny and Jane are both working very hard — learning to think mathematically, which is the foundation for all future success in maths.

Concrete maths

Many of the experiences which look like play in the infant school, and may continue well into the juniors, are really just the concrete base a child needs for any mathematical thinking. All this time he needs plenty of concrete experiences — things he can actually do, see, touch, handle. Sand and water play is not "babyish," shopping is not "fanciful," doing cookery is not "unnecessary" under the guidance of a skilled teacher. At first, of course, there will be many children who just want to play about with these things because they have not been lucky enough to enjoy this sort of experience in pre-school days. They simply want to find out what can be done with these exciting new materials and playthings. But the teacher will be watching and recording just how all her children play, and waiting for the crucial moment when the "play" can become "work," taking on a sudden interesting meaning which will lead to further experiment in number.

Steven, five, recorded his experiments with sand, with a drawing of a mug and a container. "We wanted to find which one was the biggest," he wrote, with his teacher's help. "We filled them up with 16 spoonfuls of sand in the mug and 30 spoonfuls of sand in the container, so we found out that it was the biggest."

Shopping play always fascinates the children, and in a good school you can watch the teacher turning this natural interest in shopping to good account. The five year old's early "pretend" shop soon becomes a separate activity, with the teacher guiding and suggesting and lending a hand where necessary. "Let's have a supermarket," say the children. "All right," says the teacher. "You build your supermarket over here with these boxes and planks. And how about a bank next door, for us to get money out for shopping?" The Post Office comes in useful around Christmas time, when there are busy young school "postmen" delivering cards from class to class, and Post Office "staff" issuing stamps and envelopes to customers and counting out change. One school I know exchanges letters with another school, and the Post Office comes in handy here. Another has "adopted" a ship, for which again the Post Office is in much demand for the sending and receipt of letters; the seamen regularly correspond with the pupils at the school.

Most modern primary schools own a cooker; some classes may even have one each. Children already know about cooking from watching Mother at home, and, if they've been lucky, helping too. At school they will progress from making rather grubby grey pastry and inedible cakes to the real thing: writing recipes and following them, weighing out ingredients, working out their cost. "Debbie and I made these fairy cakes ourselves," I was told by two seven year olds at a little country school I once visited. "And we've written out the recipe in case you'd like it." One London primary school I know takes it in turn for a small group of children to cook complete dinners for another group every day. And even when a school does not possess a real cooker, cooking can be done on the "no-bake" system; fruit bars and sweets can be mixed and made, involving a great deal of mathematical work with measuring, weighing, sharing out amongst the class, and working out the cost, not to mention writing and reading the recipes.

Quite soon in his schooldays your child will be using a balance, something which always fascinates the young. He will be weighing up one set of objects against another, and setting things out in order of weight. He will also be learning measurement — perhaps at first by pictures. One infant class had a child's picture on the wall, showing a large giraffe, with other pictures of surrounding objects and animals stuck on with adhesive paper. "A monkey is short to a giraffe," Kevin had written beside his stuck-on picture. Stephen had done the same with "a pigeon" and Terence with "a car." In a term or two these same children would be using the measuring tape and recording their discoveries. They would be standing under a tree in the playground, wondering about its height. "How do you measure the height of a tree?" There's a problem worth considering, and one which will need plenty of mental agility to work out.

Measuring can be brought into many activities; using ribbons to compare and measure different lengths; measuring the waists of children in the class; covering surfaces for floors in the dolls' house (area), measuring "all the way round" a circle (circumference) or round a rectangle (perimeter). Children enjoy using their own hands and feet for measuring with, or pacing distances out in the playground. Time will also be learnt. At first it will be, as in pre-school days, "after dinner" or "before tea;" then the class-room clock will be noticed, and children will learn what the hands say, and make clocks of their own. Later still, they may be making graphs and recording their discoveries in words. In the junior school, these records will be put to good use, and often combined with other topics to make a comprehensive survey of an experience or a situation.

The metric system

One point we have to consider in schools just now is the effect which decimalization, and later, perhaps, the whole of the metric system, will have on our children. This idea is of course new to us, but children are already taking it in their stride, and have begun confidently to learn the new system alongside the old. To children, usually, it is nothing but a blessing, for decimalization is helping them to cope at a much earlier age and much more readily with money sums. Ten seems to a small child the natural basis for counting. After all, he has ten fingers and ten toes; his body is certainly "decimalized." To group objects in patterns of ten is a logical "next step."

To the young, maths will be much simpler in that there will be no essential difference between "money" and ordinary number. Conversions by 12 or 20, which worried us so much in the old days, will now be a thing of the past to our children. Now, too, when they go on to decimals proper, these are simply a normal continuation of experience.

Structural maths

Structural maths

Many schools have special sets of materials which are used by
the pupils, from the time they first come into the class-room —
structural apparatus of one type or another, or, as somebody
once referred to them, "maths you can see." Your child may
very well be using one of these specially designed sets. What are
they for, and how can they help him?

One of the first educationists to use apparatus of this kind was
Maria Montessori of Italy, who long ago realized the value of
"maths you can see" and worked out a complete system of it
for the pupils in her schools, still used by many teachers today.
Other systems are much more recent. One of the best known is
the Cuisenaire system of rods, the usual set consisting of ten
unsegmented rods in different colours, which small children
love to handle and play with, and with which they soon begin to
experiment in number relationships, not by counting but by
measurement. A pink and a yellow rod, for instance, set end
to end, match in length one long blue rod. If you take away the
pink, you get left with the yellow only, alongside the blue.
If you take away the yellow, you are left with the pink only.
This is, virtually, an experiment in what, later, a child will know
as addition and subtraction.

A head teacher using Cuisenaire reports that the rods have
aroused great enthusiasm. Children of seven are learning multiplication and division facts, he says, without using tables at all,
and understand cubes and squares; they are already able to
record in different number bases and invent equations.

A very similar system is Colour Factor, though here the
colours are interrelated ; multiplying by 2, for instance,
increases redness; multiplying by 3 increases blueness. "I thought
my cup was full," says a head master who has used Colour Factor
since 1961, "when children began to tell me alternative ways of
tackling calculations, but I now regard this sort of thing as
commonplace."

Other schools use the Montessori sense-training material,
which comes in a huge variety of blocks, number rods, beads,
pegboards and so on. Teachers find they can use the correct
terms from the first; even under fives enjoy using exciting new
terms like cube and prism, and some of them even manage

pentagon and hexagon. One Head using Montessori apparatus admits that he hated maths when he was at school, but now, he says, "I learn with them and share their enjoyment." Another system is Stern, consisting of blocks used with pattern boards and trays, by which children discover simple number relationships and also relate lengths to numbers by counting the blocks. Then there is Unifix, which uses interlocking coloured cubes which can be plugged into each other and unplugged again; and Avon, pieces of varying shapes with number symbols printed on the backs. A further popular system is the Dienes multi-base arithmetic blocks (usually referred to as MAB) where children use blocks, "flats" and "longs" and can work from bases other than ten.

Which of these many systems, if any, is in use at your child's school will depend on the preferences of the head teacher; some prefer one, some another. But most seem to agree on the value of this type of approach, using carefully planned material with which children can at first play informally, and later begin to make mathematical discoveries for themselves.

You can almost see a child learning by these methods. One boy played with the ten and nine blocks of the Stern system for three afternoons and then told his teacher, "It was a good game and always happened." That "always happened" was the secret of his first mathematical discovery; it had become part of his experience, and he had discovered it for himself, not had it told him by a teacher. Therein lies the difference between what a child is told and what he finds out.

Two children playing skittles used cubes from a Unifix box to record their scores, fitting them together in a long "train." Then they laid the trains side by side to find out which one was the longer, and finally counted up to see who had won — another discovery. Billy, who is a retarded child and who in another type of school would have found maths both boring and difficult, came up to his teacher in great excitement and announced breathlessly, "I know what three thirteens are — it's three of the tens — that's thirty — plus three of the threes — that's nine — so it's thirty-nine." This child possibly couldn't have learnt in any other way than through "maths he could see."

Some of this structural apparatus can be bought by parents, together with a manual, and parents sometimes wonder whether it is a good idea to use it at home with their children. Most teachers do not favour this without consultation with themselves first. If your child is not learning this way at school, and you want to help him by using the apparatus, it is wise to have a word with the school first to make sure that what you do is not going to clash with methods used in the class-room. It is also, of course, necessary that you yourself fully understand the manual.

One point which worries parents from time to time is that structural systems which use coloured rods or blocks may not be of much use to a child who is to some degree colour blind: roughly about 8 per cent of boys, but less than a half per cent of girls. This is certainly something to be watched, and some schools already test for colour blindness if they use such methods, either to teach maths or reading. Usually it does not prove a serious handicap to a child, because he will be learning, not only by colour, but by handling, measuring, comparing as well. But if you are in doubt, or if your child seems unhappy using these methods, then a test by a doctor might be advisable.

In the junior school

As children go further up the school, their work will become more complicated, but generally, until the time a boy or girl is eleven or twelve, the type and quality of mathematical experience needed at school will remain the same. Children will simply go on to further discoveries, rapidly becoming more experienced in communication, not only through discussion and conversation about what they are doing, but by recording their discoveries and the solutions of challenges they meet. They will do plenty of individual and group research, in maths as in other fields.

Shopping activities will continue to be enjoyed, but they will become more ambitious. One school had the idea of bringing out a class newspaper and decided that its contributors ought to be "paid." They then set up a bank to issue the "cheques" and deal with the newspaper's finances — quite successfully, too.

Shape and size continue to fascinate. Two girls, both 9, made a floor pattern from card and sticky paper, using coloured diamond shapes. One said, "If you fold any diamond shape in half, you will find they are symmetrical," to which the other added, "If you put them on top of each other they look like a lot of boxes."

Graphs will be important. As the proverb says, "One picture is worth a thousand words," but children of junior age will be learning not only to look at such pictures but to interpret them, as pictorial records of what they have done. They will discuss something attempted, and having arrived at some conclusion or formulated a principle, they will write down in essay form, or otherwise, what the graph represents. Sometimes this is done in individual books, at other times as a group project.

Julia, who is ten, made a graph of Birthday Months in Our Class. She wrote, describing the frequencies of the recorded birthdays. "Most are in December. If, however, my survey had been on the whole school, the results may not have been the same. If I carried out the survey through the whole of England, the figures may be different again. I have used only a small sample . . . and it would be wrong to say, 'December is the month when most children are born'."

There is almost no end to the topics which can be explored by children in this way. One teacher listed the work in graphs done by his children at various ages. They ranged from heights, names, types of pets and bedtimes, at the infant stage, to "How Saturdays are spent," "Towns near our school," "Top ten TV shows," "Makes of cars" and "Favourite authors" in the junior school. It is easy to see, from this, how maths spills over into other areas of learning – a far cry from the old time-tables with separate periods for geography, history, reading and writing which must never overlap.

Mathematical work can apply to such varied studies as rainfall and tides, plant surveys, music (one group made a graph of the lengths of chime bars in a scale), social surveys (how much pocket money and how it is spent), and history (graphs of population during Plague times were made by a group of juniors interested in this).

Yet another group of boys and girls became involved in the possibilities of triangles. These, they discovered, could make things rigid. This led on to the discussion of the function of triangles in buildings, and in bridges, the use of the arch, the shapes of girders and so on – fast approaching the science of engineering. Some of them went on to research into the development of the bridge, and the uses of the arch in architecture, and found themselves deeply immersed in history. It is when teaching reaches this level and children, as here, respond with the whole of their interest, that you begin to feel that "learning" is like a tree whose branches strike out in many directions, growing and increasing over the years.

Does all this mean, then, that the old "computation" has been discarded? To many parents it may seem so. Teachers do not appear to be concerned to the same degree with facility in "saying your tables;" yet are not these necessary as a child goes up the school and faces exams where quick computation will be required?

Most children who have been taught to build up tables for themselves acquire the necessary "table facts" almost as second nature, because they have seen for themselves the truth and the constancy of them. Nevertheless, they may still find it useful to memorize tables, and most teachers give practice in this, either as short daily exercises, or as "homework," which a primary child quite often enjoys doing. But there is no longer the old emphasis of chanting tables like magic rhymes; the children understand what lies behind them, and when they do not know a fact, they know how to find out, using their concrete material to help them. When a child really finds it difficult to memorize tables, some schools allow him a means of recall such as a simple reckoner, just as a bad speller can have recourse to a dictionary. After all, why should a child be held back in his maths just because he finds memorizing difficult?

In the old days, a child never "went on" to multiplication until he knew his tables. Now, things may be reversed; understanding the operation of multiplication comes first. Indeed, it can come without knowing "tables" at all, simply by experimenting with blocks or similar material and finding that "the answer is the same all the time." It is another case of "maths you can see."

Your child will still, probably, be doing sums, though he won't call them that. He may call them "mathematical games and puzzles," as do the pupils in one junior school I know, where cards with questions and suggestions, following the natural sequence of the mathematical ideas the children learn, are available for the children to work out, and are often used by the pupils during "free choice" time during the afternoons. Such assignment cards, to be used by individuals or groups, may be about number patterns, volume, area, shape, place value — all kinds of ideas. But they are "structured" by the teacher, who knows what the children want and are able to learn, and at what point to push their desire for "discovery" further.

One thing which is quite different from the old style of mathematical teaching is the importance attached to "open ended" maths thinking. Questions may be set, but there may be more than one possible answer; in marking, they may not be the kind to which a teacher used to put merely a cross or a tick. Very often children will be asked to find out "what happens if . . . ," — something which can often be answered in a variety of ways. It is this type of flexible thinking which is important for modern mathematics, and is likely to become even more important in the world of tomorrow.

It has another effect, too. Thinking like this is encouraging to the child. It gives him the feeling of mastery and success, and takes away the cause of so much mathematical failure in the past, the fear of "getting it wrong." This is a very definite advance in our concept of education, and one which has a way of spilling over from maths studies into other aspects of a child's life at primary school. The pupil who is confident that maths is something within his ability will become confident in other areas of learning as well. Many parents and teachers see this as the most rewarding thing of all about modern methods of mathematical teaching.

A small boy who had recently changed schools put it well when he said that the maths at his old school were "out of a book, into a book." "Here," he said, "they show you what's behind adding and subtracting; it's exciting!" Showing children "what's behind" the use of number, as of language, is really the basis of education in the new schools of today.

The magic of books: through reading, children extend their imagination and vocabulary

6
Children and language

What is reading? What a silly question, some parents might say. Of course it's "knowing your letters," learning to interpret a book that is put before you; that's reading.

But in a deeper sense than this, what is reading all about? It has been defined, in a memorable phrase, as "a meeting of minds upon paper." If you think about this, you will come to understand the basic nature of what is going to happen to your child when he starts to read. He is going to be able to communicate with someone else's mind; he is going to "get through" by means of the printed or written word.

Reading, then, is much more than just making out words in a book. It is a means of communication. The first job in teaching reading is to help a child to communicate — to use language intelligently. And this means going farther back even than books and print, to conversation. It is important for parents, too, to realize this, for it explains why, when a child first starts school, he is not always immediately presented with a book and told to get on with it. Many five year olds go cheerfully off to school on their first morning convinced that they will come home having been taught to read; indeed, some are quite disappointed if they don't. "I thought they were going to teach me to read," said one little girl after her first day at school, "but nobody did."

Many parents still believe that a child should start straight off by "learning his letters," and are sometimes seriously worried because their children have been at school a whole week, perhaps a whole month, and "still haven't started reading." But the picture changes if we regard reading in its deeper sense, as communication. Children have to know what reading is for, and to feel the need of it, before they begin its technicalities. Many of them also have to be given the urge to communicate, by being encouraged to talk and to listen. Teachers have quite a job these first few weeks, sorting out their pupils from all kinds of homes and backgrounds, and though some of the children obviously, will have come from families where conversation is meaningful and books are a familiar sight around the house, others will not have been so lucky. So for these first few days or weeks, the main objective in the infant school will be to encourage all the children to talk, use words, and listen to each other; and then, to discover how spoken words and sentences have their counterpart in print.

A child who has been read to frequently at home, perhaps belongs to the children's department of the local library, goes to the library "Story Time" once a week, and looks at picture books of many kinds, will clearly be in a better position to start reading than one to whom words and books mean nothing. There are numbers of five year olds, unfortunately, who come from homes where there is scarcely a book to be seen, or where "books" mean magazines rather than bound volumes. They see Father getting his information and interest from the TV set rather than from the printed word, and Mother perhaps only buying a "weekly" for the knitting patterns. Most retarded of all will be children who come from homes where even conversation is discouraged. A surprisingly large number of children are brought up in families where conversation, as one researcher in reading has put it, is limited to phrases like, "Shut up," "Sit up," "Eat up" and "Wash up." Language here has ceased to be anything but a means of telling a child what to do or ensuring that he keeps quiet.

First steps towards reading in school, then, will be first steps towards what a teacher calls "reading readiness." Using words and phrases, listening, telling news, "telling back" a story heard, discussing a problem or a discovery with another child or with a teacher — all these are essential introductions to "reading readiness" — the time when a child will be ready and keen to cope with the printed word. Only when he knows, or feels in his bones, that reading is a way of finding out something and writing a way of telling something to other people, will the printed books become meaningful to him.

In a school with a flexible time-table, or perhaps "family grouping" where children are at various stages, it is easier to ensure that each child starts reading when he is ready for it. If your child has had plenty of chances of "communicating" at home, or at playgroup or nursery school, and is already "rarin' to go ," then probably the teacher will start him pretty soon on the serious business of reading and writing.

Though some schools still take "reading" as a class subject in which everybody begins together, more and more infant schools are now allowing a child to start at his own pace and go on from there. So it may well be that instead of being given a book on his first morning, your eager five year old will be playing in the book corner, joining a group round the teacher who is showing pictures in a book or, in a family grouped school, attaching himself to someone a bit older who can already read and who later can help him with new words and perhaps even "hear" him read while the teacher is busy.

A good school will use many of these approaches to reading, and will not push a child who is not quite ready to get down to a book. Many do not reach the "print" stage till they are six; these children need the stimulation of play and lively activities, something to talk about which will make the printed book "readable." Play of this kind is not waste of time. Instead of, in that very expressive phrase, learning to "bark at print ," a child is now learning what language is for, instead of merely repeating letters and sounds after the teacher and being praised for repetition.

Starting to read

How will your child be taught to read? There are many systems in use in different schools today, and in some, many methods even within one class. Teachers often find that what suits one child does not suit another, and where there is difficulty in learning to read by one method, a flexible teacher will change to another. But it is important for the parent to find out about these methods, so that a child's progress can be assessed, and so that he is not hindered at home by lack of understanding, or prompting along different lines — "how *I* learnt to read when *I* was at school."

Some teachers use the "look and say" or sentence method. Here a child takes a group of meaningful words at one jump, as it it were, either from his reading book or from cards pinned round the room or from a wall sheet. "This is our hamster," he may read on a card pinned above the hamster's cage. "This is Susan's peg." "Come and read in this corner."

Other teachers use the phonic method to start with: teaching basic sounds from which a vocabulary can be built up. "Cat," by this method, is not "see-ay-tee" but the "kuh" sound, followed by "a" and by "tuh"; and "sat" will become "suh" followed by "a" and by "tuh." The child learns by ear to group sounds together, and goes on to build a vocabulary of his own.

Most teachers combine both these methods to a certain extent, often starting children on "look and say" (which is, after all, how a child makes his first acquaintance with words in everyday life) and supplementing this by teaching sounds, on which he can build himself. Some teachers like to use "flash cards," printed with words or instructions — "Open the window," "Stand up," "Jump up and down," which are shown to the children for instant recognition. Children enjoy these recognition games, and they also enjoy games of the Snap variety ("my card says the same as yours — snap!") and many others which the teacher suggests or invents. Later, books may be given to the children, and a start made on a planned sequence of reading primers.

If your child is using a book such as the "Royal Road Readers," or the "Programmed Reading Kit" of Professor D. H. Stott, a set of games and exercises based on sounds, he will be learning along the phonic system — by ear. If he is on the "look and say" system, his books may be the "Janet and John" series, in use for a number of years in infant schools and now giving way to the "Kathy and Mark" series.

There are many other books and programmes for teaching children to read. Your child may well be using "Words in Colour," invented by Dr Caleb Gattegno (one of the pioneers of the Cuisenaire colour rod method used in mathematics). This starts by giving children the basic vowel sounds, each of which is shown on a big chart in a different colour. Altogether there are 21 charts, including 47 different constituent sounds, each of them allotted a colour or a shade or a two-tone colour, so that a child can learn consonants one by one, put them together with the vowels, and build up a vocabulary through colour, which is always reliable. Sounds in the same "family" can be recognized this way in spite of illogical spelling.

Another colour method, "Colour Story Reading," by Kenneth Jones, uses only four colours but also makes use of background shapes (triangle, circle, square) to identify sounds. Story books and records have been brought out using this method, and over 1500 schools have adopted it.

One method of teaching, or encouraging, reading is by television. The new series "It's Fun to Read" might be called the first tele-reader. In it, two puppets are introduced to the child viewer, at home or at school, and though it does not go very far in teaching reading fluency, it does start a young child off in the right direction, by showing him how to follow words from left to right, how to break the print up into separate word units, and how to build up a small vocabulary.

Still another is "Breakthrough to Literacy," a kind of card game in which the teacher has a Sentence Maker (a set of some 130 cards which can be arranged to make sentences). Children are dealt out word cards to construct the sentences of their choice, and only later go on to letter cards to shape words. There is an accompanying record of nursery rhymes, in a variety of dialects to avoid producing an "Oxbridge" accent which might be construed as the only "right" one, and a set of story books, plus a "food alphabet" to increase a child's workaday vocabulary.

What is i.t.a.?

Much the most discussed method of teaching reading, however, is the i.t.a. or initial teaching alphabet, devised by Sir James Pitman, and now becoming so common that public libraries are even stocking up children's books written in the special "i.t.a." script. The core of the method is that children should not be put off learning to read by having to master the vagaries of the English alphabet, the 40 sounds of which are printed or written in something like 2000 ways. (We have only to consider the differences of the "a" sound, for instance, in *am, any, want, fall, rate, father,* and the two forms of writing and printing, upper and lower case or, as we say, capitals and small letters, to realize how perplexing all this must be to a small child.)

I.t.a. starts with a simple and purely temporary medium, a new alphabet which is just what it says, initial in that it is only a beginning, and teaching in that it is used for the specific purpose of getting a child to read. There are no capital letters to confuse him, simply larger forms of the "small" or lower-case letters, and the foundation of the alphabet is our own lower-case characters, with q and x left out and 20 more characters added, most of them versions of our own "digraphs" or combined letters (such as "sh" joined up to make one character).

In this medium a child can start his reading confidently, knowing that he has an alphabet of 44 letters, each one representing just one sound. He can't go wrong. Later, he transfers to the second stage — traditional orthography (ordinary print) or, as it is known, TO — which is not as difficult as it seems. After all, we ourselves find it comparatively easy to adjust, when reading, from upper case (capitals) to lower case (small letters), and to the child the transition from i.t.a. to TO is just as easy.

Schools using this method make many claims for it, chiefly based on the fact that it produces confidence; a child gets started more quickly and gains by being able to tackle anything written in i.t.a. without fear of failure. Some schools are more doubtful about its success, and certainly it cannot be claimed as a panacea for all reading ills. One of its drawbacks is that such an alphabet must be based on accepted pronunciation of sounds, and does not allow for local variations of speech.

However, most teachers find that for slower readers in particular, who feel themselves dropping behind and become frustrated, this method can give an added stimulus. So if your child is learning by one of the more traditional methods and does not seem to be making any progress, it would be worth while finding out whether he could be helped by tuition in i.t.a., even if it means asking for a change of school.

Your child's vocabulary

Small children love trying out new words, and it will not surprise us now to find five and six year olds using a vocabulary which, years ago, would have been considered above their years. Some first reading books are still very limited in this matter of vocabulary; limited, not only in the number of words used, but in the content of the reading matter, which is often too middle class and "cosy" for the workaday world in which most children live. Recently, some different types of first readers have been brought out, which are more directly linked with an ordinary child's (especially a town child's) experience. The children in these reading books may live, not in a cottage in the country or even a suburban street, but in a block of flats; mother may work at the factory, the family takes the washing to the launderette, and Dad brings home fish and chips for supper. Certainly it is a good thing to provide a wider field for a child's early reading, to introduce words which he already knows, and tie up his reading with real life. And there is no doubt that first reading books, on the whole, have tended to be too unadventurous in their vocabulary and subject matter, and made children bored by constant repetition of, "This is Spot, our dog. Look at Spot. Spot, come here."

Another innovation in first reading books is to provide subject matter which fits the age of the reader. Many boys and girls of seven, eight or nine still cannot read with any fluency, yet the books they have to use in the class-room are those published for a five or six year old, with more babyish interests. Today there is a move to provide, not only more interesting and realistic textbooks, but books which will appeal to the older child, who still may be a slow reader. Books about cars and football will sustain the interest of a boy, say, of eight or nine, who as yet cannot master the vocabulary of the early readers, but still needs something sensible and suitable to read about. This is the lure of the "comics;" they have stories which really move, where there is some action; and the same rule should apply to school reading books at each stage of a child's learning.

Learning to write

Reading and writing cannot be separated, for they are both means of communication. In most infant schools they will be going on at the same time. A child usually recognizes his own name in print in the very early days, and likes to see it written. "This is Peter's book," the teacher may write on his drawing book, and soon Peter will be wanting to copy what she has written. Soon he will be helping to keep a chart of the weather, or writing notes for another child to read, about what the goldfish or the hamster should be given to eat, or writing out a recipe for making scones in the cookery corner. He will perhaps make his own book — "My family" or "The house where I live" — illustrating it with drawings and paintings, and reading it aloud to a group of children, or to the teacher. This two-way flow of reading and writing is important, for it means that a child knows what language is for. The two skills are mutual; both spring from conversation and discussion, and both are needed for everyday life.

In the more traditional school, the reading lesson and the writing lesson are separate; a child learns to read by the book, and learns to write by copying letters and sentences. Great stress is laid on neat writing, careful copying from the board, and the correct formation of individual letters. Children are taught how to compose their sentences, when to put in capital letters and commas, and of course how to spell correctly.

I was looking the other day at a piece of writing done by a boy of five at a northern infant school. He was bursting to get down on paper his ambitions for the future — "When I grow up." This is what he wrote:

"I like to be a barber cose you Get a Rayt Lot of Moniy and in yor shop you Get a Rayt Lot of PePeL in yor ShoP Thay av bayds I will Put bill krim on that her I like to cut mashtashase Sum men will brinG ther little boys to av ther little boys her kut I like to Put sheyvinsowP on ther fayses and sheyv it off I want to be a barber naw I will Giv them shotbackandsayd kruwcot sqerneck I seL rasabLads shaving Loshan shavinsowP and biLcriym I shaL chath the Men 3 shiLig and boLd men 2 shiLig and boys 6 Pans."[1]

Rubbish? Misspelt, badly punctuated? Yet in two years' time the same boy was imagining his own experience as a shepherd boy to whom the Christmas angels appeared:

" 'See, a light.' Hastily we covered our faces with our arms . . . Sheep stampeded down the hill and I ran after with my staff. But I stopped half way down, surprised to see an angel on the hill top, saying, 'Unto you a king is born, a savior, a

[1] *The Excitement of Writing*, ed. A. B. Clegg, Chatto & Windus, 1967 pp. 111, 112.

Lord of Light, who shall bring peace on earth, goodwill to all men.' I wanted to round up the sheep but somehow I had to go strait away to find this new king. I fixed on my cloak, picked up my staff, and a lamb. At first Jacob would not come but soon he changed his mind . . ."[1]

This little boy attended a school where the teachers encouraged children to write creatively. In other schools, children of five, six or seven might still be writing laborious but technically correct sentences about Spot the dog or Puss on the rug, or about the flowers in the spring. Here, the children from the start let their writing take them where it would: they did not confine themselves to "easy" words, nor did they adhere to the stock "subjects" which traditional teachers all too often set. Children in this school treated both reading and writing as means of communication, tools for expressing all the busy and rewarding experiences they met with every day, or could imagine or dream about. Teachers here did not wait for the children to "learn" to spell or punctuate before allowing them to write. Instead, they encouraged them to write first, and "acquire" spelling and punctuation as they needed it. The result? Lively descriptive writing such as that above, at first barely intelligible, but progressing steadily and surely towards the work quoted just two years after; strong, simple prose needing very little in the way of "correction" but containing the same vitality as the work done in the first year.

What is the point, some parents ask, of "not bothering" about spelling and punctuation at the start? Wouldn't it be better for a child to begin as he means to go on? The short answer is that the child who is pestered to write accurately and correctly at the expense of his own enthusiasm just doesn't get started at all. His urge to get things down on paper becomes dulled if, first, he has to learn to spell, to punctuate, always to be accurate. But by capturing a small child's natural interest in "writing a story" or "telling" about something he knows, a good teacher can lead on gradually towards a more accomplished style, better punctuation, better spacing of sentences, correct spelling. She can help the young writer to take a pride in his work, spelling well because it is more communicable that way, using proper sentence structure because people will understand what he means. There are many

[1] *op. cit.,* see footnote opposite.

105

examples from schools to show that a child who starts with
enthusiasm, even if he is a bad speller, gradually acquires good
spelling as he goes along. The subject is not neglected, but
instead of doing endless "spelling drills" and learning by heart,
he is helped to "remember" the right spelling and to look up
words he needs in a dictionary, or to ask other pupils or the
teacher. In the same way, learning to punctuate need no longer
mean boring sessions on "the use of the comma" or "when to
put a full stop." By writing a lot, and reading a lot, and talking
work over with the teacher and fellow pupils, a child can "pick
up" accepted punctuation and style much more readily than if
he tried to learn sets of rules by heart.

That piece of work by a seven year old child was far more
imaginative and interesting than it would have been had the
teacher not allowed him free rein in the earlier years. It is easy
for parents, as well as teachers, to criticize a piece of work done
by a child in the infant school, mis-spelt and blotchy, with a view
only to its accuracy — missing, thereby, all the excitement and
enthusiasm which went into its writing. And there are many
families where children's early writing, brought home with pride,
is pulled to bits by unimaginative parents on the grounds of
carelessness: "They never teach them nowadays how to spell and
punctuate. Just look at this!"

Yet children encouraged to write freely are producing far
more lively work, and more of it, simply because they are un-
afraid; they are confident that they can write, as they talk; and
they are open to experiences. Modern teaching tries to draw
those experiences from them, to give them the tools by which
they can put them into words — their own experiences, not
pale copies of something else they have read or heard. Listen to
this poem by a little girl of ten in a Yorkshire mining area
junior school:

>   The Candle
>
> White polish; sour milk,
> Delicate finger wrapped in cotton blanket.
> Star growing, bigger, bigger flickering in darkness,
> A great Lord, now a humble person bowing,
> Golden crystals, dark eye,
> Slowly, flowing, running, milk.

Faint glimmer of hope, trying to enlarge itself.
Black burned pie; all beauty gone.[1]

Poetry comes as easily as prose to an imaginative child like
this, from an ordinary experience which she has learned to express
most movingly; all the more spontaneously because she was
never, in the early years, badgered to "write correctly" or "get
the spelling right," let alone "make the verses rhyme." Nowadays, teachers are less concerned with rhyme (though it has its
place) than with the poetic quality and shape of a child's verses.
And it is far better to let a child like this write as she wants,
using the pattern that comes naturally to her, than to tie her
down to traditional rhyme — the conventional "Spring"
rhyming inevitably (and oh so dully!) with ring and sing and all
the rest. Many people would consider this Yorkshire child's
poem to be as sensitive, observant and individual a piece of verse
as any emerging from an adult poet's pen.

The teacher at this school says that children learn to write
by writing, and writing creatively; "what they need is opportunity." Here, pupils do not work at something called
"composition." They experience things, and then try to find
the words that express them. Sometimes this is done by
individuals alone, at other times, perhaps a group or a whole
class may share some experience (firework night, or walking
through dead leaves) and try together to think of suitable words
to describe it before they turn to their own work. The teachers
do their best to help them use their senses, and their imaginations, to see and hear things vividly, and to transform them
into meaningful words. This does not, as many parents fear,
imply sloppy, poor, inaccurate writing; rather the reverse. More,
not less, attention is paid to the way a child writes and the
vocabulary he uses, but the "drill" has gone, and the teacher
watches instead for opportunities to help him improve his work
as he goes along.

Stories and record keeping

In the modern infant school, once a child has mastered the
elements of forming his letters, he will probably start by writing

[1] *"The Excitement of Writing"*, ed. by A. B. Clegg, Chatto & Windus,
1967, p. 53.

stories. Most children enjoy hearing stories read to them, and are ready and eager to write their own. As one teacher puts it, the more they hear and listen, the better they write; so stories are told them over and over again, and poems read to them, so that certain words and phrases stick in their minds and "become" their own. When at last they begin to write stories, in large books made by the teacher, and using unlined paper and thick pencils, they are supplied with any words they need, and helped to choose the right words for themselves. Spellings which prove hard to remember are taught incidentally, and largely individually or in small groups where there is evidently a common need. Many children in our primary schools choose "writing" to do in their free time periods, just because they enjoy it; from being a burden, it has become a pleasure. Children, too, like to read to each other, and to the teacher, what they have written. All writers need readers, and this two way flow between those who write and those who read is very important in the infant and junior school.

But there is another kind of writing which children need to do; that is, recording. This may be at first a simple statement of fact, "I made this model." Or it may be an every day necessity, "These sweets are two for a penny." In the infant school, and increasingly in the junior school, a child taught along modern lines will find himself writing both creatively and informatively, writing stories, poems, essays for his own satisfaction, and writing down records of things he has done, discovered or made. As the child goes up the school, more time will probably be given to recording as a daily occupation, and will take the place of the note-copying associated with the set history, geography, science or nature study "lesson" of the past. Except, of course, that it will not be dictated by the teacher, but will come from the child's own mind, and be expressed in his own words. "Just as we learn to talk by talking, we learn to write by writing," one junior teacher said. And so, in the junior school, practice every day in writing both creatively and scientifically helps pupils to perfect the skills of good style, grammar and spelling.

Your child may be asked to describe, first in words, later on paper, the result of a simple scientific experiment carried out at school. Or he may write about shells he found on the seashore, or discoveries he made while visiting an old castle or abbey in the neighbourhood. This kind of writing has to be practical, accurate, clear enough for other children to understand the point of it, so grammar and spelling may be brought to his notice particularly, clear handwriting praised and suggestions made to improve the general layout of his work. A child who might have resented, in the old days, having to "go back and do it again," will not usually mind being helped to rewrite a piece of recording work more clearly, so that it becomes a worthwhile project, fit to include in a class-room "book" or hang on a wall sheet. In this way, the child is rather like an apprentice craftsman, who will welcome suggestions on how to use his tools and take a pride in improving his performance. Indeed, child and craftsman have much in common; each has to learn how to work well, and for this each needs practice.

The best practice a child can get in good writing, whether stories or records, is through wide reading. As one teacher put it, children should learn how to "live with words." The more they read, the better their own work becomes, so a plentiful supply of books is of first importance, whether they come from the school, the home or the local children's library, to which any child can belong, and which often visits local schools with an inviting display of books for children to read.

Helping spelling and punctuation

Some children are naturally, it seems, poor spellers, and need additional help. Here, a dictionary can be a great incentive. Today's teachers see that each child makes his own personal dictionary as he goes along, and where someone finds spelling particularly difficult, he can be provided, quite openly, with a junior dictionary and shown how to "look up" his spellings, just as in the mathematical field, someone who finds it hard to memorize table facts can be provided with a simple reckoner.

A dictionary is not regarded, however, merely as a spelling check. It is, as one teacher put it, "an exciting storehouse of words" on which children can draw. In one junior school, whether they are good spellers or bad, all girls and boys in the third and fourth years have their own dictionaries as a matter of course; these can be consulted at any time during writing or reading. All children, too, have a personal vocabulary book into which they write "difficult" words, or words they might need for future use, and which they find interesting. The poor speller or the child with little flair for words can be inconspicuously helped here by a good teacher; his personal dictionary can be amplified, and frequently checked over, so that he has more than the usual fund of words, and spellings, at his disposal. It does not hurt him, of course, to take home a few special "spellings" each day or week to learn and make his own, but he is not held up to ridicule as a bad speller. And the fact that he is given the means to improve his spelling brings the confidence he needs to catch up with the rest of the class.

One particularly bad speller, a boy who simply could not master words or express himself at all freely, was encouraged by his teacher to make his own "Dictionary for Martians." This was a work intended to help possible visitors from Mars to cope with learning the English language. Tom got immensely interested in this idea of helping such a strange creature to read and write the more common words of our language, and soon produced a creditable Martian dictionary in which words were spelt out with great pride and accuracy. The other children helped him in this, and before long Tom's use of words had improved out of all recognition. Nagged at for poor spelling and poor vocabulary, this boy would never have mastered language. But given the idea of words as a useful tool, he made progress almost immediately.

Punctuation depends very largely upon listening carefully to the spoken word. Beginners in the infant school do much of their early punctuation, like spelling, incidentally, and by ear. They come to "hear" where to put the full stop at the end of a sentence, and what a comma is for. As they go up the school, wide and intelligent reading usually helps to form a kind of pattern in the mind, so that they come to know the appearance of capital letters and semi-colons and all the rest. A teacher may occasionally take a discussion period for talking specifically about punctuation, when a common difficulty seems to have arisen, or she may correct individual mistakes as she reads what a child has written. Where somebody seems to find the punctuation of a sentence perplexing, she will provide special help. She will also see that a poor writer gets plenty of unobtrusive chances to write messages, send letters, or put up notices about the school. If, sometimes, a poor writer instead of a good one is chosen to write the "thank you" letter to the Fire Station or the farm to which the class has just paid a visit, it is surprising how much care will be put into the work. Such a child can be helped to punctuate correctly and set out his sentences readably, because his is a special mission, a responsible job which he has been given to do. Looked at this way, helping the poor speller or writer takes on the form of guidance and encouragement rather than punishment or nagging, and the child responds more readily.

Feeling at home with words

The main point about reading and writing today is that a child shall come to feel "at home" with words, whether they are his own or those of another author. For this reason, stories are read and poems studied by children in the primary school which are classics of their kind — sometimes far ahead of the material which one associates with the young child. "Does a child really understand that?" one might ask, when some author usually reserved for adult reading is introduced into the primary class-room. The answer is that most children take in far more than they actually understand; they can learn to enjoy literature and to share the "feel" of rough tree bark compare with the gentle even if they do not understand every word of it.

In the same way, they can reach heights in their own writing which surprise many adults. Teachers today try to encourage creative writing, based on the emotional and sensory experiences a young child meets from day to day. How does it feel to look up through the branches of a tree to a deep blue sky? What patterns do the boughs make? How does it feel to touch the bark? How does the "feel" of rough tree bark compare with the gentle feel of grass, or the feel of a handful of earth rolled round in the palm? What sounds can a child hear? Street cries on market day, the shrill whistle of engines, the clanking of wheels, the rattle of milk cans at a railway station, the tiny sounds of birds and animals in the woods — all these can be listened for, and words found in which to express them. Trying to get a child's own personal response to these things down on paper is not an easy way out for the teacher; it demands a very real and close relationship with the child. But what comes from these creative writing periods can be really worth while.

Here are some of the experiences written about by juniors: Market Day, The Dodgems, Some gipsy caravans, Inside the control room of the power station, Snowball Fight, Our street at night, An Hour by a Rough Sea, My Dad, My Pets, The Organ. But whereas a generation ago, "My Pets," for instance, would have been a neat little composition containing the usual facts about animals, listen to what this boy of ten has to say about his two hedgehogs:

"When they where in a ball they look like black pincushions with hundreds of black and white pins the wrong way round in them."[1]

Spelling and grammar-wise, perhaps, not perfect, but what observation!

But does all this wide reading and lively writing, ask some parents, make for success in examinations? When we were at school, we did a series of lessons in English Grammar and Comprehension. In the first we had to answer questions like these: What do we call a mermaid's father? the home of a horse? someone who sells fish? In the second, we had to read through a set passage and then "tell it back" briefly — not to show whether, or how, we had appreciated its contents, or been stirred by its imagery, but just to indicate whether we had understood the words in which it was expressed.

We also did a series of exercises on the use of words, filling in blanks such as "Night is to day as Moon is to ———." We knew how to punctuate a given unpunctuated sentence (though it did not always follow that we could punctuate our own). We also knew how to form words from each other, following (or trying to follow) the vagaries of English spelling: how to add "ing," for example, to words like smile, fulfil, enjoy or go.

Fortunately, these old "eleven plus" types of English tests are rapidly on the way out — where any written test still exists — and examiners too have come to see that the scoring of marks for this and that matters less than the general ability to express

[1] *"The Excitement of Writing"*, ed. by A. B. Clegg, Chatto & Windus, 1967, p. 74.

oneself clearly and vividly, using a fair vocabulary and retaining a reasonable standard of grammar and spelling. In this, the teachers themselves have had a say, for it has been largely due to their insistence on the useless, time-consuming nature of the old type of drills and exercises that such tests are on the wane. But the fact remains — and it is an encouraging one for parents to whom the new teaching methods are unfamiliar — that children who have had few, or even no, formal lessons in grammar can still reach standards quite as high as those who have been through the mill of spelling, punctuation, sentence structure and the rest. And children who have read widely and according to their choice — whether or not the books were "standard" readers for their age — are far in advance of those whose aquaintance with literature was confined to a series of reading books or a number of "potted" classics.

The position has been well summed up by one teacher who has taken many groups of children through their English lessons; it is nonsense to take "English language" as a subject at any time or stage. It is better by far to forget about the subject, and concentrate on getting child-conscious, language-conscious teachers working with children in all sorts of ways, and "what's written up or talked about is English,"

What parents can do

When we really understand what a teacher is trying to do in the realm of language we can readily think of ways to help a child at home. The most obvious one is through conversation. Encourage your child to talk, to explain what he is doing when he makes a model, to tell you about his painting, and later, to exchange ideas, even if they seem immature to you. He can only develop ideas through talking about them. Then, of course, access to books is important. He can build up his own personal library, with the aid of Christmas or birthday money or book tokens; browse with you through the children's department of the local bookshop (some towns have special Children's Bookshops which are even better); and join the library, where the junior section is often surprisingly lively, perhaps with displays and talks, a Book Club and a chance to meet children's authors face to face.

Writing, too, can be encouraged at home. Quite young children enjoy "helping" mother by writing out the shopping list; an older boy or girl can keep a holiday diary; and a family or group of friends can run their own newspaper, with contributions from all. Many children compose poetry at school; suggest they do the same at home, and let them write out their poems and share them with other people. Working together, like this, both home and school can help children acquire the mastery of language, not only for its own sake but as a tool for the necessary job of communication.

7

Discovering the world

The world of today's primary school is an exciting one for most children. It is a kind of microcosm of the world outside; a world in miniature, where they can try their hands at many subjects and become involved in many activities, besides the traditional three Rs. To many parents, however, the big change from a time-tabled day (which they could understand) to one which is, apparently, very flexible and very free, presents difficulties. Where have all the lessons gone?

Granted that our children learn about language and maths, what has happened to all the other subjects we used to have at school? When we ask a child, "What did you do in history today?" or, "What country are you studying in geography?," quite likely we are met with a surprised stare. "History? What's that?" "Geography? We don't do any." Is this really true? Don't they study these subjects any more?

We are also puzzled, sometimes, by the new terms the children use. What, for instance, are the "environmental studies" which seem to take up so much of Jane's time? What is this "music and movement" which Peter enjoys so much? One thing is certain; it is unusual to find a child who is as thoroughly bored as we often were, doing our nature study or history or scripture. Most of them seem to work just as hard, if not harder, than we did, looking things up in dictionaries or reference books, going to the library to find out something for a "topic," making models or painting in their spare time. They are certainly busy; but what on?

The reason for discarding so many of the familiar old "subjects" is tied up very largely with the new approach to a child's day at school. Teachers nowadays try to work with the tide, as it were, instead of against it; they use a child's natural zest and curiosity to further his studies, rather than forcing him to sit down and study a set subject at a set time. It follows that

the old "time-table" has gone by the board in many schools, and
with it have gone, apparently, many of the subjects which used
to divide up the day. One thing blends into another, so that it
is hard to give a separate name to the many activities a child is
involved in.

Teachers are slowly acquiring a new understanding of the way
a child learns; and not only in the infant school but in the
"juniors" too, the old history, geography, scripture and all the
other "lessons" are being abandoned in favour of what Whitehead
calls "the seamless robe of learning" — learning that goes on all
the time, and is all one.

Your child is no longer being called upon to follow, closely,
a single thread of knowledge for forty minutes by the clock, but
instead to study the whole fabric, where all the various threads
are woven together into a pattern that makes sense.

Environmental studies

This is why history and geography, for instance, have been
merged into what a modern primary school often calls
"environmental studies" — the study of the world which lies
about a child, to be seen, touched, investigated, discussed, in its
present and in its past. The present world — geography — may
even be found right on the child's own doorstep. Instead of
starting gaily off to learn about "Children of Other Countries,"
John may be encouraged to begin discovering the country in
which he lives, and about which he has a natural curiosity.
When he makes a plan of his local housing estate, or builds a
relief map on the class-room table of his particular bit of coast
or mountain or valley, there is his geography taking shape from
the places around him. The same with history; instead of going
straight back to William the Conqueror, he may start, once more,
right on his own doorstep, by going to look at that old house
which is being pulled down to make room for the new supermarket, or asking Grandad about his memories of village life
forty years ago.

Finding out about a child's own environment — the history
and geography of the place he lives in — sometimes starts in the
most unlikely places; seldom nowadays, out of a book. In one
town where housing estates seemed to have buried all the past
beyond recall, a headmaster of a junior school took a small

group of pupils to find some old cottages about which he had vaguely heard. It was rather in the nature of a voyage of discovery; the headmaster himself had never seen them, and didn't know precisely where they were. All he knew was that they were under a preservation order, and represented the original country village out of which the new housing estate had sprung.

The only clue to the mystery was the name of the road down which they were walking. "This is Meadow Lane, Sir," said one small boy. "But there isn't anything old here. I live here; I know."

But in fact Meadow Lane really had been a meadow once, and tucked away behind the neat rows of houses, these children and their teacher at last found three ancient cottages, which had once looked out upon the lost meadow. The end cottage was in process of being modernized, and the children could see for themselves the old beams, with their wooden pegs, the lath and plaster with which the walls were built before the days of bricks and mortar, the thatch which covered the ancient roof. Later, the people in one of these old cottages invited a party of juniors inside, and the children felt the thrill of walking on the old paved floors where the inhabitants had trod centuries ago, and of exploring the baking oven set deep into the wall.

Questions, of course, came thick and fast. Why didn't they have electric light? When was electric light first introduced? Why did they have to get water from the well? Wasn't there any piped water in olden days? Why did people have to bake their own bread? What did they eat? How did they live? Where did they work? The past was rapidly coming alive in Meadow Lane, right in the middle of a modern housing estate; and the children went excitedly home to read books in the library, ask grandparents, consult maps, find out in every way they could about the history on their own doorstep.

Another class of juniors in a seaside town were interested, each summer, in the large number of tourists who came to spend their holidays there. Some of their parents took in summer visitors, or helped in hotels. One boy, whose mother kept a guest house, thought it might be a good idea to make a local guide book for visitors — "People are always asking Mum what to go and see." So he and his friends got together to collect information about places of interest, and how to reach them. Helped by the teacher, they first discussed in detail what places should be included in the book, and then found volunteers to make a large-scale map of the town, and smaller maps taking in neighbouring areas of the coast, with notes about things to see and do. This led to a host of questions about local geography — how the cliffs came into being, what was the origin of the famous "hole" down which visitors liked to peer to see the tide rushing in below, why the coast was indented with tiny bays, where the river came from which ran into the big estuary. When the guide book was completed, it was duplicated and given to visitors who happened to come to the school, and to the parents of children who wanted it. In the process of making it, these pupils had learnt an enormous amount of local geography which had been triggered off, not by pages in a book, but by their own spontaneous interest and suggestions.

Indeed, there may be no formal history or geography books at all in your child's junior school desk, though there will be many books of all kinds, about all nations and ages, on the library shelves or in the reading corner. Environmental studies or project work, too, may spread into a whole morning or afternoon, or take up large blocks of time during each week, instead of being confined to certain periods. Teaching may go on right outside the school premises: at the museum, at the local fire station, in the docks, or in the market, where small groups of children may go together with, perhaps, a list of questions to answer, or things to watch for and record in a booklet later. Film and radio programmes may also be used, or children may listen to a talk by a visitor — a policeman from the local police station, somebody's dad who is a farmer, the Junior Librarian from the municipal library, or an overseas visitor with interesting things to tell about his own country and its history — all these may be enlisted to help with children's studies. Besides these visits and talks, children will be doing research in the school library, constructing models, taking part in projects, perhaps making up and acting a play — approaching history and geography from a number of different angles, and getting deeply involved in the subject. Though they may not know the dates of the kings of England ("And why should they?" asked one teacher." They can always look them up in a book. I can't remember any of the dates I learned at school!"), they will be

storing up plenty of knowledge of a really useful kind, and
though they may not be able to rattle off the names of capes and
bays, their geography will be a living thing, concerned with the
real world. When eventually they systematize all this knowledge —
during their secondary schooling — they will have acquired
enough sense of time and of causality to set these things down
in a formal manner. But the junior school is the place for
discovery.

All this, of course, does not involve less work from the teacher,
but usually more. Parents who think that teaching "environmental studies" along these lines is a soft option for the teacher
do not realize the hard work that goes into a well-planned term.
Even with such a free and flexible programme, a class teacher
needs to know the capacities of the children, and the range of
work they have been covering during the year before. Certain
arrangements have to be made — visits planned well in advance,
books ordered from local libraries, speakers invited to talk —
necessitating an ordered progression of work, of which the
teachers are very conscious even if the children are not. A good
teacher, too, will have to be responsive to the children, and
know when to abandon a topic which is not "catching on,"
when to pursue a worth-while project further, and when,
perhaps, to switch to an entirely different one when some child
comes along with a new and exciting discovery that stimulates
all the class — "Miss, a big lorry's just come round the back, with
cement for the new swimming pool; can we go and watch?" Is
there the beginning of an idea here — about building, about
materials, about craftsmanship — which could be followed up,
as it were, on the crest of the wave of the children's own
enthusiasm?

Music making

Of course there will be certain times during the week when space
will be available for the definite practice of certain skills, such as
music or games. There will be times when the big hall is empty,
and can be used for "music and movement" by a large group of
children; days when the playground is free for games. Both
these activities — making music and developing physical skills —
call for regular practice, and in both great advances have been

made recently in recognizing the part they play in the life of the child at school.

When we learned music, it was still something of an "extra" subject, which nobody took very seriously except the dedicated few. Singing was for everybody, except the tone deaf children who "hadn't any ear" or "had no sense of rhythm." Instrumental music was for the gifted, if enough instruments could be found; the ordinary child was not expected to shine in this, unless he took additional lessons out of school. Some children were considered "musical" and played at school concerts. The rest just got along as best they could.

Today, teachers see music as a rightful and basic part of every young child's life. If a baby can enjoy banging a spoon or beating a saucepan lid with a piece of stick, if a toddler can be responsive to music and want to dance when he hears it, then surely music must be inborn in every child. Curiosity about sound and enjoyment of it is part of everybody's makeup. It has nothing to do with whether a child can sing nicely in tune, or learn to play an instrument.

Music, in fact, as one county music adviser once put it, is like falling in love; it depends on propinquity. "A child," he said, "must get close to the stuff, so close as to be excited by it." When he hears music, however young he is, he instinctively wants to take part; and so you find, in the nursery and infant school, children enjoying music with their teacher — dancing to it, or moving their bodies, then copying her rhythmic clapping, tapping, or knocking on a desk or table, then making elementary music themselves by singing, clapping or tapping out some musical "sentence." Using just their own voices and hands, quite young children can produce a miniature chorus and orchestra with a rhythm they enjoy.

Later, they will learn to master simple instruments: percussive ones like the tambourine or drum, or what a music teacher would call "melodic percussive" ones such as the xylophone or chime bars. Soon they find they can make up their own rhythms and melodies. This is the sort of "creative music" that primary children can all enjoy. It does not depend on musical skill, or the ability to play or sing with any special talent before an audience, though there are always some who can readily acquire such a skill, and will be helped to use their gifts to the full. But for the large majority of children, the important thing is simply to enjoy making music in every form they can think of, with all the instruments a school can beg, borrow or buy.

Most infant schools have percussion bands, with things to bang and things to shake — probably home made. Even upturned flower pots of different sizes, hit with some kind of striker, and old washing-up-liquid containers filled with rice, can be brought into play. Many junior schools have recorders, which are simple, inexpensive instruments with real musical possibilities; some can provide tuition on the guitar, or on string or wind instruments, and even a school without any instruments at all can have fun with singing — often taught, not in the traditional manner by a teacher at the piano, but with the teacher perched on a chair or stool, singing a song she herself enjoys and letting the children naturally "join in:" all the better if she can strum a guitar.

Children readily invent their own themes, and at first the teacher will listen to these and write them down, as she does when a child first makes up a story or verse. In this way, children become acquainted with musical notation. Most parents would be surprised at the range and variety of musical composition which goes on in many schools. In one, a group of older infants became interested in a picture book called "Noah's Journey," and soon got involved in setting it to their own music, some contributing vocally and others with simple instruments. A year later, these children were equally excited about the story of David and Goliath. They made a giant model of Goliath which stood in the school hall, and using voices and instruments, made their own music for the story — soft music for the shepherd boy scene, fierce warlike music for the battle, and a glorious song of victory to finish with. In another school, a village school, the children composed a cantata based on poems they had written themselves about the birds seen and heard near their homes and school.

Radio and TV programmes on music making are also very popular in many schools. A record player or tape recorder can create a great deal of pleasure and interest, too. Where expensive items like these cannot be provided, many parent—teacher associations can usefully get together to buy one, and if a project like this is afoot in your child's school, it is well worth the effort of supporting it. Record players and tape recorders are not "frills" which a school can do without; they can provide a very real stimulus for the children, and foster individual music making and appreciation.

If your child is seriously interested in playing an instrument, some primary schools lend instruments on a termly basis, for a boy or girl to try out, and in country districts the Rural Music Schools will lend instruments and help a child to get tuition. Many counties are now developing instrumental playing, not only in the secondary schools, but in the primaries as well, and may run Saturday morning music schools to which young musicians can go. Any family with a promising child of eight or nine would do well to talk things over with the primary school with a view to obtaining really good tuition and the chance to participate, perhaps, in a school or county orchestra and to join in Saturday classes. Often a better musical education can be given through the school than through an individual teacher. This is particularly worth bearing in mind, should you have a boy with a really good singing voice; for it might lead to the child's acceptance by a choir school, offering the very best in musical education alongside the general curriculum of a prep school.

Drama

Music in a child's life is closely associated with movement and drama, and will often go alongside dramatic work or mime. The years when junior schools produced an annual play for the benefit of parents, with only the best actors performing, are gradually giving way to a more constructive view of drama as something belonging by right to every child, and with no undue emphasis on "good performance." Indeed, drama is more an opening up of the personality than an acquiring of talent.

Drama in most primary schools will take the form of improvisation, very often to the stimulus of music. Children have vivid imaginations, and take very little persuading to "play out" a scene or situation, in an unscripted and informal way. An inventive teacher can drape a piece of material over a chair and say "Can you see the king's throne?" and of course everyone can see it, and wants to be the king, or a courtier, or a prisoner coming to beg for mercy. Stories or suggestions for improvisation come naturally from children, too, helped now and then by the teacher. Properties are usually of the simplest: one drama teacher picked up a battered old eastern jug at a junk shop, which became, in the course of one week, treasure from a wrecked ship, a magic jug which could turn you into stone, and a container for boiling oil which some ferocious cannibals poured over their reluctant victim! Curtains and drapes of all kinds are used, to turn clothes horses into houses, and children into witches and princesses. Movement is often set to music, with home-made drums or shakers, or the school's supply of chime bars or glockenspiels, or a record player is used.

Is all this a waste of time? Couldn't the children do their play-acting just as well at home? Parents who prefer the old type of scripted play or the careful "elocution" lesson might consider that though these things may have their place from time to time, the real value of drama is to allow an outlet for a child's imagination and emotion. Behind these apparently free and formless drama periods lies something much deeper than mere play-acting: the development of sensitivity to a situation, and awareness of others.

Children learning to move and speak and use music in improvised drama are loosening up and gaining in confidence as they could never do if compelled to act in a scripted play. They are frequently playing out their own dreams, fears and problems, working out, as it were, typical situations in their own lives, giving them an airing and finding ways of dealing with them. It is this which makes drama so worth while in the primary school.

Physical education

Music and movement will be very closely linked in the modern primary school; nevertheless, certain times will be allotted for physical education, when children can escape altogether from the bounds of the class-room and use the school hall, playground or field freely to enjoy various forms of movement and learn the skills for games. Great advances in physical education methods have been made since the time when "drill" or "physical training" used to figure on our time-tables, with formal exercises for developing various parts of the body in turn — "hands on hips," "head turn," and all the rest.

Instead of emphasizing posture for its own sake, children are now introduced to movement as something flowing and continuous, developing naturally from the free play of the nursery school, through the more skilled and adventurous games of the infant school, to the physical "education," in the widest sense of the word, of the junior school. Teachers are now concerned with the production of good carriage and poise, and the development of skills in simple ball games and athletics, which will be the basis of future work in the secondary school.

For the physical education periods today, children generally strip down to vest and pants, and run out freely in gym shoes to move about and enjoy themselves informally for the first few minutes. If apparatus is provided (and this may mean anything from the full equipment of a school gym to simple improvised "props" such as planks and ladders, or just the banks and trees of the village school field) they will choose their activities freely at first, encouraged by the teacher, just as they were at nursery school, to experiment at their own pace and trust themselves in climbing, jumping or balancing as far as they feel able to go. Safety precautions, of course, are observed, but today's teachers are much less inclined to expect everyone to go at the same rate, or to demand more of a nervous child than he feels capable of achieving. Physical education time is meant to be enjoyed.

Later in the period, children will probably come together for various games: chasing and tag, ball activities of many different sorts, skipping, running, jumping. These, with older children, will lead up to the teaching of the skills needed for football, netball, cricket or rounders. Games like these are sometimes taught in the primary school, when children are around nine or ten, and teams may be made up, but at this stage there should not be too much in the way of competition. Athletics, also, will be begun, not aiming at technical perfection, but teaching a child good style: how to run well, acquire an easy throwing action, or jump a rope with confidence.

Primary children nowadays are regularly taught to swim, and if your child's school has no pool of its own (many are now beginning to acquire small learners' pools which are not too expensive and which can be used for the first stages of swimming), there will be weekly visits in summer to local baths. Swimming is now considered an essential activity for every child, and since from the nursery stage most children have already acquired a certain amount of confidence in the water through paddling and playing about, there are few of the old fears of "going in" which used to leave so many young swimmers trembling on the edge.

You can do quite a lot yourself to help your child learn to swim, by taking him to local pools and making swimming a family pleasure. At school, on his first visit to the baths, he will not be forced to begin swimming straight away, but will be encouraged just to enter the water, and, holding onto the rail, develop confidence by jumping up and down, ducking his head, and kicking up his legs. The next step will be to join others in simple group games and races in the water — "crocodiles" or "boat races," throwing and catching a ball or ring, and then gradually breaking away to move about more freely in the water. By this time a child is ready to learn the proper movements of swimming — to glide towards the rail, then to swim, later to glide and plunge from the steps and finally to dive from the side into deep water. By nine or ten, most boys and girls have made friends with the water and learnt to swim reasonably well.

Science for juniors

You may be surprised to find that science, which used to be considered a secondary school subject, may be an integral part of your child's work even at the primary stage. Can young children really get a grasp on science as early as this? Of course, if you think of science as it used to be taught in the secondary school, with books, problems, and carefully written accounts of set experiments to "prove" this or that, none of it would come into the junior range. But science properly means investigation, and in this sense it is of the very stuff of the junior school, for children between seven and eleven are investigating all the time.

Although there may be no science teacher as such in the junior school, there is likely to be a great deal of scientific investigation going on. It will be sparked off by experiments prompted, probably, by things the children themselves find and bring to school, or ask questions about, and they will not be told facts, so much as encouraged to find their own answers to problems of "How?" and "Why?" by doing further experiments and discussing the results.

You might very well go into a class-room and find a group of boys and girls playing with water — seeing what happens when you drop a stone into it, or an alka-seltzer tablet, or a few grains of soap flakes. Or you might find them examining a heap of stones and pebbles picked up on the beach, observing their size, shape and colour. Others might be interested in a collection of various polystyrene oddments — weighing them against each other, finding out about the properties of this strange and fascinating material. Why does it insulate against heat? Why does it float? Still other children might be doing experiments with wind-borne seeds: one class in a rural school climbed the church tower to find out how the seeds dispersed. These spontaneous experiments, undertaken by the children with the materials they find about them, might be called a kind of random sampling of science: they cover a wide field, but lead on to further enquiry, and stimulate scientific thought in a number of ways. Later, in the secondary school, they will acquire more pattern and shape, and be more formally recorded.

By finding out the answers themselves, children are laying a good foundation for their later work. Their "science" may seem unplanned, yet already, at this stage, the teacher will be providing the right terms for the children to use, and suggesting ways of recording — pictorially, in graph form, in writing or merely in talk and discussion. One of the first attempts to encourage this kind of science in the junior school was the Nuffield Junior Science Project, which originated in 1964 and was tried out experimentally in a number of schools in various parts of the country. Like Nuffield maths, it required a set of publications to show teachers how to use the scheme, and courses were laid on to brief certain staff to act as leaders in their own areas. Much pioneer work has been done in the various Teachers' Centres, and today Nuffield science is being introduced into more and more junior schools by local authorities, or integrated into the kind of scientific enquiry which was already being begun by progressive teachers with groups of junior children.

Primary French

Primary French

Will your child learn French at his primary school? Many
parents are surprised to find an eight or nine year old beginning
a foreign language, something hitherto reserved strictly for the
over elevens, and the brighter ones at that. Yet today, primary
French is no uncommon thing: about one fifth of our junior
children are already learning it.

The pilot scheme for teaching French to children between
eight and thirteen was sponsored jointly by the Schools Council
and the Nuffield Foundation, and Nuffield French has spread
to schools all over the country. But there are also other schemes.
London, for instance, has one of its own, whereby certain
primary schools are linked with local secondary schools for
continuity; the non-specialist teachers who take it at primary
level have attended courses at the Institut Français in London,
been to evening classes with language laboratories, and spent
several weeks at Besançon University in France.

How are children taught at this age? Certainly not by books
and grammatical exercises, but by a carefully planned programme
which leads a child, at an age when he is unselfconscious, into
the way of *thinking* in French. It is French by doing, playing
and talking, rather than by reading or writing. Some schools use
radio, films and tapes, some use the record player, some nothing
at all but the teacher's own leadership and initiative.

French schemes are many and various, but all have one thing
in common: they aim to get children interested in the French
way of life, ready to join in games and singing, to exchange
simple conversation, without recourse to rules or grammar. As
one teacher has said, "French today is something one lives and
does, rather than learns. "On these lines, children from eight
upwards listen to French voices, play games in French, go
"shopping" in French fashion, and gradually feel their way into
the language through play and real-life situations.

In one school, for instance, I watched a group of eight year
olds playing at "department stores." They had cardboard cut-
outs of clothes — shirts, ties, socks, coats — pinned to the rails
of a clothes horse, and one child was acting as shop assistant
while the rest shopped in turn, in French, for some article of
clothing. These children were thoroughly enjoying themselves,
playing first, learning only secondarily, and yet quite efficiently.

Even if they didn't remember all they learnt, they were getting
the "feel" of another language. In a tiny village school I
watched a bunch of youngsters playing a traffic game, also in
French. They had model cars and pipe cleaner dolls, and the
teacher had made a cardboard background of a typical French
market square. A street accident had just happened, and a toy
ambulance was rushing to the rescue, the children chattering
gaily in French all the time. In another country school I found
children singing French songs to their own recorder band; and in
yet another, there was a "French corner" alongside the nature
corner, and children were examining French picture books and
handling French coins there.

The purpose of teaching French so early is not to get all
children speaking accurately in a foreign language, but to make
them feel "at home" in it before they reach the age of self-
consciousness when they do not like to try a new sound or use
foreign phrases for fear of failure. Giving a child confidence is
important; it is something which can easily be done, in language
teaching, at a very early age (some private schools teach five
and six year olds a foreign language alongside their own), so it
seems a pity to waste any chances.

Some teachers carry their French methods even further.
Talking to one London headmistress in a very crowded and
underprivileged district, I was surprised to find how far the
language teaching in this school went. No child here was surprised to be casually addressed in French by anyone passing
through a class-room, or to be asked to stand up and sing a
French song. Further, this school was linked with a French
school in Boulogne, and exchanged day visits with the French
pupils. Such visits were open to any child who wanted to go on
them; the English pupils were paired with corresponding French
ones, attended morning school with them after arrival (Boulogne
is only a few hours' travelling distance away), and were taken
home to lunch with French families. Some, later, even exchanged weekend visits to each others' homes.

What happens to early French learners when they go on to
secondary school? There may, of course, be difficulties if there
has been no continuity between junior and secondary schooling.
Headteachers report that the French speakers usually learn new
material more quickly and with greater confidence, but benefit

from repetition of what they have already learnt, so that it is not too difficult to bring all children to the same level. The great need at the present time seems to be to provide enough teacher training for those who want to introduce a foreign language early into the junior school; if this can be done, nothing but good would appear to result to the pupils.

Art and craft

What will your child be doing in art and craft? Today these subjects are not differentiated so much either from each other, or from the rest of the school day. One of the joys of an integrated programme for teaching is that painting and drawing, modelling, building things, making things, come into so many activities. All the same, there will probably be certain stretches of time when art work can more easily be done, or the art room and art materials are more readily available; or perhaps a child will choose "art" in one of the free-choice periods.

The great feature of today's art teaching is that art is thought of as being experienced by the child, rather than "taught" to him. It is something he does naturally, a way of expressing ideas and feelings, in fact a language — to some children, inarticulate in other ways, perhaps the most important language of all. Primary children are not "taught" correct ways of handling their tools, but allowed to experiment in colour and form, with help from the teacher where it is needed.

Young children usually enjoy colour and pattern and texture, and can be taken quite far along the road to appreciation of these things, apart from what they do themselves. I once watched a junior teacher mounting an exhibition of "blues." He had assembled on a table a number of different objects and textures, in varying shades of blue: the deep blue of a peacock's feather, blue cardboard, a "drape" of blue velvet, a length of pale blue silk ribbon, a dark blue glass bottle, some blue tissue paper. When the children trooped into the art bay, there were cries of delight — "Look! It's all blue!" Then suddenly the teacher introduced a round bright orange into his "blue" group, and there was a gasp of appreciation at the contrast. Here were children learning to enjoy colour and texture, to be sensitive to it in a way they would never have done by studying colour charts or mixing paints in the old-fashioned art room.

Children extend their art and craft in many directions.
Besides painting on large pieces of paper, or at easels, using big
brushes and lots of colour, they enjoy doing group work —
friezes, backgrounds for puppet plays, costumes for dolls,
collages from pieces of tinsel, bottle caps, velvet and silk. I have
even seen a beautiful lacy collage made entirely from torn bits
of newsprint, begged from a local printer's, and glued onto a
background.

The elements of pottery may also be studied, using a school
kiln (or one shared with a neighbouring school or an art college).
Or they may do woodwork or needlework, girls as well as boys
trying their hands at both, and tie-dyeing, roller printing and
lino cuts are also much enjoyed. But these crafts will probably
spill over into many periods of the school day. In one infant
school I watched children busy making a spacecraft, from a
huge assemblage of junk — cardboard boxes, pieces of tin, bits
of string, silver paint, corrugated paper; the result was acclaimed
by the whole school, and given a place of honour in the porch
where visitors and parents could see it. In another junior school,
as I came into the entrance hall, I found beautiful pressed
flower arrangements, carefully mounted under glass, decorating
the walls; whilst at another London school, a large "dragon"
came walking towards me, propelled by a couple of children
inside a really fearsome creature made from a green curtain,
with papier maché head and scarlet eyes and tongue, all ready
to take part in a play about St George.

Who can say whether this "craft" applies to history or English
or drama or science or nature study? Everything runs together
into a purposeful whole. So, while your child may well bring
home some good paintings and enjoy seeing his work displayed
on the wall, he does not need to be "good at art" to enjoy all
that goes on at school. All the time he will be increasing his
awareness of what can be done with shapes, colours and materials; whether he "succeeds" in producing works of art is really
beside the point.

At home you can help him by appreciating his efforts, not
criticizing or continually asking what his pictures represent.
They represent something to him, whether it is an object or just
an emotion or an experiment in colour. Materials such as crayons,
paint, charcoal, oils, poster paints, paper and glue, if available at

home, will spur him on to further experiments. Above all, don't
be disturbed if your child gets himself messy whilst painting or
making things; all artists and craftsmen are messy at times — it is
part of their job. Provided a young artist works in an overall,
and clears up after himself, then there will be little to worry
about. If you can put this idea of the artist—craftsman before
your child, it will help him to take a pride in his work and his
tools, and keep his art or craft materials tidy. It is well worth
putting up with a bit of mess occasionally if the experience can
do so much for his education in the widest sense of the word.

Religious education

There is yet another field which your child will explore at school,
whether or not he is supported in it at home, and that is
religion. Unless you issue definite instructions that he is not to
receive such teaching, he will join in Assembly every day and
a scripture period (or religious education period) at least once a
week. Strangely enough, although in many other countries
religious education is felt to be the province of the home, and
may actually be banned in the schools, as in America, over here
it is the one subject which every school must teach, according
to the Education Act of 1944, and it is obligatory by law for
children to take part in Assembly unless parents apply for their
children to be withdrawn. The syllabus is called the "Agreed
Syllabus," devised by each local authority on the combined
advice of concerned bodies — teachers, clergy and others.

Is it a good or a bad idea to have compulsory religious
instruction? True, a parent has the right to remove his child,
and many Roman Catholics and Jewish families do so; yet there
are other parents who would rather keep their children's
religious education in their own hands, or who do not wish any
such instruction to be given at all, who nevertheless respect a
young child's sensitivity to being "different" and do not like
to embarrass him by insisting that he be taken out of the class.
Many parents, too, would like to see religious education
enlarged to include teaching about other faiths besides
Christianity, especially since, with so many immigrant pupils in
the schools, there is now a better chance than ever for children
to learn about each others' faiths in a friendly atmosphere.

Recently the World Congress of Faiths, on whose council are Christians, Muslims, Jews, Buddhists and Sikhs, declared its support for religious education in schools on the ground that "the spiritual dimension is a part of human experience," but at the same time supported courses in world religions at colleges of education, so that teachers could include the study of other religions as well and teach them with imagination and sympathy. It may be that this is one of the major issues facing education today. Some schools are already very successful at helping children to develop their natural instincts of reverence and wonder, without indoctrination at all. I have watched Morning Assemblies where the children themselves take the service, make up their own prayers of praise and thankfulness, show paintings or pottery that they have made, to add to the beauty and pattern of life, or describe the joyous experiences of a day in the country or a visit to the sea. There may be little formal religion expressed in these assemblies, but the children are really involved in them in a deeply spiritual way. But there are undoubtedly many more where the singing is perfunctory, the prayers unintelligible, and the pupils bored; where the real purpose of Assembly seems to be for the Head to issue notices and deliver warnings. As one child aptly put it, "It's not prayers at all, it's just 'Don't do this' all the time!"

Training teachers to take Assembly or scripture periods purposefully and sincerely is essential, and of course can only be done where members of the staff are serious in their own beliefs, or at least sympathetic in attitude to the young child's innate sense of the wonder and mystery of life. Bible stories without explanation, hymns that may even frighten a child, or doctrines thrust down the throats of a class without attempts at discussion, can do more harm than good. So parents are quite right to question religious teaching where it is unsympathetically given, by teachers who have received no help in presenting it to children. Those who care about it will see that children receive teaching at home, church or sunday school, and many will be glad to find that they are mixing at school with children of other faiths. Some may choose to send their children to a church or denominational school where teaching will be along their own lines, and to an application like this local authorities usually give a sympathetic hearing. It is less easy for

parents who are agnostics, or actively antagonistic to religious
teaching, to get their children either out of Assembly or away
from a church school into a non-denominational one. Certainly
there should be freedom of choice; but at the moment, the
whole subject of religious education and Assembly in schools
is very much in the melting pot.

How you can help

With such a wide field of learning, what can parents do to
supplement their children's work at school? Don't leave it all
to the teacher; however numerous the activities going on, children want and need support from home — somebody to take a
personal interest in the many things they are doing and learning.

Every family should make opportunities to go out together —
to visit places of interest, explore the countryside or the town,
perhaps do a bit of brass rubbing at an ancient church, or make
a special excursion to a castle or cathedral. There are often local
activities going on — special concerts for children, holiday
lectures at museums, junior membership of photographic, art or
natural history clubs — about which details are usually posted up
at the Town Hall or in your local library. More and more towns
are initiating Arts Centres for young people, where children can
go in their leisure time to take part in painting, model making,
drama or puppetry. Or, if your children are not the "joining"
type (some children just do not like clubs or centres), they may
enjoy having a bit of garden of their own, keeping a pet, or
taking up a personal hobby like stamp collecting. All of these
activities will start them asking questions, consulting books,
comparing notes — the stuff of which true education is made.

Television too, widely used, can be a great interest, as well as
providing entertainment. But pick your programmes together
with your child, and watch them together, if you possibly can;
it is the "togetherness," with the chance to discuss and comment
afterwards, which makes the difference between intelligent
viewing and passive "box watching."

Don't forget, either, to give your child opportunities to meet
people, to talk to visitors about their jobs or experiences, share
in family hobbies and of course family holidays. You don't
need to travel abroad, either, to widen your child's horizon;

there is plenty to see in this country. Family life can open up wonderful possibilities where parents are aware of their children's developing interests and are prepared to go along with them and perhaps suggest more. Just as a good teacher makes a better pupil, so does a lively home produce a livelier child, all the more ready to learn, explore and grow.

Men at work: a playgroup leader helps with carpentry activities

8
Special help for special children

No family can expect to get through without some problems occurring in early childhood. Every boy and girl is bound to meet difficulties along the way; indeed, part of the process of growing up is learning to meet and resolve such difficulties. When these are minor, they usually solve themselves. A new teacher replaces an old one; family tensions lessen; or a pair of spectacles, or a slight hearing defect remedied, is all that a child requires to put him on a level with other children again.

But there are other problems of a deeper kind, or a more permanent nature. The toddler who is so very slow to talk, and then cannot pronounce his words; the seven year old who can't be made to go to school; the nine year old who still cannot read; or the young trouble-maker whom nobody can manage — these are the children about whom parents and teachers understandably worry, and for whom specialized help is needed.

There is, too, the increasingly growing category of children born with recognizable physical or mental handicap. Babies have better chances of survival today, but with this goes a steady increase in the number of children growing up with congenital defects, and needing special care and schooling.

It is fair to say that with proper handling, suitable education and the sympathetic support of the community, even severe handicap can be greatly lessened. In many cases of physical or mental disability, or severe deviation from the norm, a vast improvement can result once a correct diagnosis has been made. The trouble is that so often the handicap is never detected. John is called "dull" when all the time he is merely a little deaf. Susan is called "naughty" when her extreme restlessness and lack of co-operation is due to a dysfunction of the brain called autism. Philip is relegated to a C stream in school when he is a brilliant boy with intelligence so far beyond the rest of the class that he has stopped trying from sheer boredom — for genius can be a handicap, too. Half the difficulty may be that a child's trouble goes undetected till it is too late.

There are, also, other problems which can beset the most normal family. A child becomes ill and is hospitalized for six months. What is to happen to his education? A father is ordered overseas, and the children go with him; what can they do about schooling? Or a job necessitates constant moving around; how can continuity be preserved when children are always changing schools? Any of these contingencies might befall your family. The difficulty is to know just what help is available, and how it can be applied to your particular case.

Mental handicap

Let us begin with mental retardation, which sometimes shows quite early in a child's development. This can happen to anybody; it does not reflect on the intelligence of the parents. "My baby doesn't sit up yet." "Mine's so slow in walking; he doesn't seem to want even to pull himself up." These are signs that a doctor should be consulted. True, there is a wide variation in the ages at which these "landmarks" occur; but if your child is clearly months behind expectation, and particularly if he does not appear to *want* to do these things, then medical investigation may be necessary.

Sometimes, as in the case of mongolism, retardation can be detected at birth. In other families, it takes a little time to show itself, and it may not dawn on parents, till the doctor confirms it, that their son or daughter is severely subnormal in intelligence — that is to say, by later tests, with a quotient below 50 compared with the "norm" of 100. Such a child used to be labelled "ineducable" and assigned to a junior training centre under the Ministry of Health, or allotted to a hospital for subnormality. Happily, today the position is different: no child is dubbed "ineducable" altogether, and responsibility has been transferred to the Ministry of Education, where of course it always should have been. The whole process of "ascertainment" as subnormal, in fact, needs complete overhaul. Children do amazing things when environment and teaching is specially adapted to them; and with the chance of nursery school experience and the advance of new techniques, many a subnormal child has surprised both parents and teachers by developing at least to the point where he can lead a satisfying and comparatively independent life, even if he can never, in the academic sense, "learn" very much.

One point worth remembering is that even if your child has been "ascertained" as severely subnormal, it is possible to get a reclassification later. This is quite within the rights of parents to demand, just as it is within their rights to appeal if they suspect their child of having been wrongly classified. The whole business of "labelling" a child is fraught with difficulties, so that in no case should a family take an official ruling as final.

Another point of great importance is that all these children benefit enormously from mixing as early as possible with others. For them, nursery experience is particularly rewarding. Fortunately, many more nursery schools and playgroups are opening their doors to subnormal children alongside the others, or giving over certain afternoons to them, using the nursery materials with skilled staff. Places like Stevenage, Bury St Edmunds and Wandsworth have been leading the way in this, and there is every sign that the number will increase as nursery staff and playgroup leaders come to realize how vital this experience is to the handicapped child.

The main source of help for the family of a retarded child is the National Society for Mentally Handicapped Children, which has recently opened the first "retardation centre" of its kind in the world. This movement is concerned with retardation in all its aspects — medical, educational and social — and its new centre in London has grouped within one building the various specialist services which can help such a family. Parents can receive advice, children can be assessed, and certain teaching can take place which is having remarkable results. In the Centre for Learning Disabilities here, there are two "talking typewriters," the most recent invention to help a handicapped child to learn. This machine, based on a very involved computer, talks, listens to and responds to what a child says, praises his efforts, and can even sing (in six languages), and present pictures which help him to learn at his own pace. This is possibly one of the most outstanding breakthroughs yet devised in the education of the mentally handicapped, and here at the Centre this and many other experimental methods are being tried. There is also close liaison with the College of Special Education, which trains teachers to help retarded children.

There is still a great shortage of specially trained teachers; it has been estimated by Stanley Segal, founder of the College, that out of the quarter million teachers in charge of ordinary children, at least ten per cent should be specifically trained for this difficult and demanding work, to cope with the children who need them. There is also a shortage of special schools and units all over the country. Probably the best step for the family of a retarded child to take is to seek, first a nursery school which will give him a "head start" until about seven, and then constantly have his position reviewed so that he can receive definite remedial help, even if it means crossing administrative zones or even counties to get it.

What about children who are not severely subnormal, but still cannot keep up in an ordinary class, the slow learners, or in educational terminology, the "educationally subnormal," with intelligence quotients between 55 and 75? The trend today is to try to keep such boys and girls, where possible, within the framework of the ordinary school, but at the same time offer them remedial teaching in small classes or units. The least useful form of such teaching is the "bottom stream" of a ruthlessly streamed primary school, where a slow learner soon realizes that he has been labelled "backward" and gives up the struggle. But in a sympathetic school there may well be an Opportunity Class, where there is no stigma on a child's mental ability, but an atmosphere of cheerfulness and confidence, with the aim of getting him back as soon as possible into normal schooling. In such units, children are not kept away from the others, but encouraged to join in where they can — in music, dancing, drama, art or games, which all children enjoy, whatever their intelligence, and which can provide such valuable outlets for self expression. Or they may be taken out, at certain times, from their normal class and given individual or small group teaching in the basic skills, together perhaps with children from neighbouring schools who also need special help.

There are special schools for the educationally subnormal, both day and boarding, where it is felt that a separate environment would help. Here, all the staff are trained for this type of work, and the pace is gentle; there is no comparison with other

children's standards, and for certain boys and girls this is undoubtedly the best arrangement. Just occasionally, too, a local
authority may help towards the fees at an independent school
which will provide the calm, unhurried atmosphere that a slow
learner needs; some of the schools of the Rudolf Steiner
Fellowship are particularly sympathetic here, with their freedom
from examination strain. But financial aid is not at all easy to
obtain; it demands great perseverance on the part of parents to
get "the County" to help in these cases.

The maladjusted child

There is another type of child who also appears to be a slow
learner, though in fact he may rank quite high in intelligence
tests. This is the maladjusted or emotionally disturbed child,
who cannot break through the barrier of his own troubles to
concentrate upon learning.

This is the sort of youngster who may be aggressive and
bullying or, as the teachers say, "beyond control." Or he may
have strange habits or obsessions, or be "full of nerves," fright-
ened of joining other children in normal play. Often he is
withdrawn and sits listlessly at the back of the class; such children are sometimes overlooked, just because they are "good"
and have no nuisance value; yet their need may be the greatest
of all. What has happened to all these children is that their inner
turmoil is so great that it blocks their power to learn and warps
their behaviour.

It is difficult to define maladjustment. As someone has said,
it is not like measles — something which you do or don't have.
So much depends on a child's temperament, the demands made
on him by his family, and the circumstances of his home life. It
is easy to think of Peter's stealing or lying as naughtiness or the
first signs of delinquency, or of Janet's inattention in class as
sheer laziness. Yet all these conditions may have arisen because
of something wrong in the inner life of these children — something which needs, not punishing, but putting right. Often, the
cause may be just circumstances, which an adult could cope
with but which to a child are overpowering. The death of a loved
grandpa, or a fear of asking questions about sex, may lie at the
bottom of John's inability to settle down at school; he has too

much on his mind to learn. When the trouble is brought into the open and talked about, the "block" disappears. In other cases the cause may have built up over the years; tension between parents, when the child is in constant fear lest Daddy leave home, or an excessive insistence on tidiness so that he is afraid to move or play freely, may both affect a child so badly that the whole family is in need of counselling if he is to get better.

Sometimes, for such children, a remedial teacher may be provided — not just someone who will help them "catch up" at school, but someone trained to cope with behaviour problems and get to the root of emotional difficulties. A one-to-one relationship with a dependable and understanding adult can make a great deal of difference to a disturbed child. Occasionally, a move to another school with different methods, or even a change of teacher, can clear things up. But where a problem does not yield to steps like these, and threatens to interfere with a child's progress and happiness, he may be referred to a Child Guidance Clinic.

The whole picture of these clinics is somewhat confused. Some of them are run directly by the education authority; every school comes under the School Psychological Service, which can obtain treatment for children needing it, and in some districts the Service runs its own clinics. In others, the local health department is responsible, or a clinic is run in conjunction with a hospital; still other clinics go by the name of Family Services, or Child and Family Guidance Centres. Their aim is to help disturbed children, and you can have your child referred to one either through the school, or through a health visitor or doctor, or by contacting the Clinic yourself, having found the address by enquiry at the Town Hall or Citizens' Advice Bureau.

The Clinics work as a team, consisting of an educational psychologist, who will assess your child's abilities, a psychiatrist, who supervises treatment, and a psychiatric social worker, who will become the family's friend, talk to parents, and generally concern herself with the background of the case. A few clinics also have a child psychotherapist for deep level treatment. The waiting list is very long, and the treatment too may take quite a time, often running into many months. On the other hand, sometimes just a chat with the staff, and advice from the psychiatrist, is all that is needed to put a parent on a different track, enable her to see the picture in a more detached way, and modify her attitude towards the child who is giving so much trouble. Often the very fact that help is forthcoming, without criticism or blame, is sufficient to give new confidence to a harassed family, and a new start for the child. In very urgent cases it is sometimes possible to bypass the waiting list and get advice for a child whose condition is really desperate.

Treatment, for younger ones, consists mainly of play — with dolls, with toy cars and animals, with paints and dressing-up clothes, through which a child often reveals what is worrying him and expresses pent-up fears or resentments. Even very boisterous or aggressive behaviour is tolerated here, by psychiatrists who understand that it may be the only way a child has of giving vent to his tension or anxiety. In some cases, a child may be sent away to a special school for disturbed or maladjusted pupils, till he has worked through his trouble and got on the right road again. Teachers at these schools are trained to deal with difficult children, and a psychiatric team is in constant touch. Sometimes an independent school may be indicated, and it may be possible for the County to help with fees; but again, as in the case of the retarded child, this is not easy, and parents must be very persistent in their demands.

If your child shows behaviour symptoms, there is seldom need to worry about his future well-being provided he is given the treatment he needs before things have gone too far. It has been estimated that at least 15 per cent of the children now in our primary schools will need special help for maladjustment at some time before they leave at eleven. Fortunately, in the majority of cases, if the need is seen, treatment can be given. It is in the diagnosis of it that we sometimes fail; so that it is particularly important for parents, playgroup staff and teachers to be aware of the symptoms of maladjustment, and ready to give the apparently "dull" or "naughty" pupil the benefit of the doubt.

The autistic child

Certain extremely perplexing children may not even respond to the usual forms of treatment for the disturbed. These are the autistics, who suffer from a condition which for many years has remained unrecognized. Recent research, however, is showing that there may be between four and five thousand of these boys and girls, with such deep problems of communication that from birth they seem unable to form any meaningful relationships with people or to respond to any normal stimulus. Someone once aptly described such a youngster as "a child in a glass ball." He can see out, but he is prevented, somehow, from joining in. Some invisible barrier stops him from making sense of the world and those in it.

Such children are recognizable by their extremely bizarre behaviour. They are often beautiful to look at, but are restless and jumpy, prone to tantrums, full of nervous obsessions such as twiddling their hair or playing with a piece of cotton or string, unable to settle down to any pursuit, and completely unco-operative with other people. The National Society for Autistic Children, which has been formed to try to help them, believes their trouble is due to delay in the development of the parts of the brain organizing the "sensory input," especially the centres controlling speech and vision. The Society estimates that at least 400 are in subnormality hospitals, simply because their condition has never been recognized officially. Countless more are in their own families, where their behaviour is so difficult that it almost disrupts the home.

But something has at least been started for them, and at present there are 23 centres, mostly in the south east, where about 850 of these children can get treatment, though at least 80 more centres are needed. Recently, the first all-age fully residential school for autistics has been opened at Slinfold in Sussex; as yet it can take only a handful of pupils, but it is hoped that this may be the beginning of recognized education for these children who are so painfully difficult to bring up at home by reason of their ceaseless nervous activity. Already it has been found that an autistic child sometimes responds well to music, and also to movement. Recently some drama students from Bristol took a group of autistic children for a movement course, where the students, one to a child, tried to "get across" to them by physical involvement — swinging them in the air, playfully fighting with them, rolling on the floor with them like puppies — and did manage to communicate to a rewarding extent. As one of the students put it, "even a foot can be made to speak;" and if these children can respond through movement, this may be some kind of a language bridge.

The gifted

Quite apart from the children we have mentioned, there is another group whose problems are also pressing, though they often go unrecognized. This is the group of gifted children, estimated as about two in every hundred, whose mental abilities far surpass the normal. Surprisingly enough, it is not always easy to pinpoint a child who is exceptionally gifted. For reasons of their own, these boys and girls may hide their own condition in the effort to be "like the others;" they may indeed even come into clinics for maladjusted or retarded children. The real trouble, of course, is that their brilliance has never been detected and allowed to develop. From the records of 10,000 children attending child guidance clinics in Eastern England from 1950 to 1966, it appears that at least 2 in every 100 had intelligence quotients of 140 or more, and yet a third of these had been referred for "poor school work" or refusal to go to school at all.

Children have many reasons for wanting to hide their light under a bushel. Family opinion may be one. It is not easy for a father to take kindly to his six year old son who is forever telling Dad where he goes wrong (and with good reason too); or for a teacher to keep up with a nine year old who is already asking mathematical questions which she can't reply to, and never taking "no" for an answer. Other children dub the genius a "brain" and don't want to associate with him; whilst older companions are at an emotional level which is still beyond him, though academically he appears their equal. Often a child prefers to give a wrong answer rather than risk other pupils' dislike by putting up his hand with the right answer every time. "I'd rather shut up in class," said one brilliant boy, "I'm tired of their calling me Prof.!"

Brilliant children, naturally, have the same emotional needs as any others of their own age, and life for them can be unhappy because it is so unbalanced. Teachers do not always help. Many brilliant five year olds may start school on the wrong foot by being bitterly disappointed at having to toe the line when all they want is to get on with learning fast. Teachers often resent pupils who ask too many questions — as the superintelligent will always do — like the six year old with an IQ of 152 who kept asking about the bulge in the cap of his milk bottle, a scientific query which didn't fit in with the hurry and bustle of getting forty children to drink their milk. And one head mistress, faced with a newcomer who already read and discussed the "Daily Telegraph" with his parents at home, sternly warned his mother that she couldn't make any allowances for him there; he'd just have to learn his i.t.a. like the rest of the class!

Another boy with an IQ of 188 actually failed the eleven plus exam and found himself in a secondary modern school because his teachers diagnosed him wrongly, whilst his brother, with an IQ of 147, had so many temper tantrums through sheer frustration that he was written off at school as just "thoroughly naughty."

How do you recognize a brilliant child at home? Usually by exceptional skill in the use of words at an early age; by originality (as someone has said, the mind of a genius doesn't run on a tramway); by early manipulative ability, putting things in the right places, making things work; and remarkable memory (the genius never has to be "told twice"). Most of all, by early involvement in some special hobby, which he pursues with more than usual enthusiasm and thoroughness for his age.

Parents can help by remembering that gifted children are still only children, needing the occasional cuddle or "blow-up" of temper to reassure them of family affection or relieve tension; also by trying to "engineer," in an unobtrusive way, chances for such boys and girls to go at their own pace: by visits to museums, holidays abroad, joining adult clubs as junior members. A typewriter or tape recorder may help a child whose ideas, as so often happens, come tumbling out too fast for him to write them down. As regards schooling, it is generally felt best not to isolate such children from others in a special school, but to give them opportunities for extra study and discussion at their own pace — "enrichment classes," as some authorities call them, for groups of gifted children from various schools, held out of normal school hours. Essex has one junior school with a special room for the gifted, where they can take their studies as far as they like under the guidance of a special teacher. This county also runs out-of-school classes at the local College of

Education, where children get the chance to meet students and staff who can help them at a higher level.

For parents, the National Association for Gifted Children offers counselling and arranges group gatherings for families, and even a summer camp where children can join in activities whilst parents exchange ideas. Properly catered for and appreciated, of course, the gifted have an enormous potential for the community, and it is rewarding to find that at last all this is not being wasted.

Some children, without being geniuses in an all round way, have special talents for music, dancing or singing. These too are gifts which should not be wasted, and usually they need special education at an early age. At present the musical education of very gifted girls and boys is not well provided for. There are only three schools where enough time and attention is given to children who need to practise many hours a day and to "live musically;" the Menuhin School in Surrey, the Central Tutorial School for Young Musicians in Hampstead, and Chetham's Hospital School, Manchester. This compares unfavourably with, say, the USSR where there are 2000 specialist music schools and another 70 boarding schools for young musicians.

Probably the best plan with a highly musical child is to talk things over with his teacher, or ask for an interview with the Director of Education, to ensure that sufficient allowance is made for practice time. For country children, the Rural Music Schools can frequently advise and help. Sometimes there is the chance for a future performer to join a local music group, or an orchestra; one such exists in Hampstead on Saturday mornings, where children from two and a half can make music along with older ones and even adults in a lively way. Most counties also have school orchestras, and, later, county orchestras for young people, and these chances lead up to the National Youth Orchestra at the secondary school stage — an organization which brings together the most talented boy and girl instrumentalists from all over the country.

If your boy happens to have a good singing voice, it is worth watching the local paper (or enquiring from the Choir Schools Association) for auditions for young choristers at choir schools, usually attached to cathedrals. A boy is auditioned at about 7 or 8 years, and if offered a place, will have his fees paid to such a school, which is run on ordinary prep school lines but with much more time allotted to music and singing. The load is fairly heavy, for ordinary work has to be done as well, and Christmas and Easter are busy times; but boys from choir schools stand good chances of gaining music scholarships at public schools or at university. Most, besides singing, learn at least two instruments at school.

Ballet schools also take pupils from about 8, boys as well as girls. The best of them give a wide education as well as specialist teaching in dance; the cream of them all is the Royal Ballet School at Richmond, but there are many others, one of the best known being the Arts Educational School at Tring in Hertford-shire. For a child going to make a career in ballet, an early start is important. It is essential to get a proper audition and sound advice by the age of nine. Stage schools also like to get their pupils early.

The physically handicapped

There is, unfortunately, a very large proportion of physically handicapped children. The whole picture is complicated, for it is not always easy to tell, at an early age, what is a permanent variation from the norm, and doctors are naturally reluctant to worry parents about what may well correct itself in time. However, in certain cases, particularly deafness, where speech may be inhibited as well, an early diagnosis is vital.

Any hearing lack can be tested at a clinic as early as seven months, and the parents of a hearing-impaired child will certainly need advice. Specialist help should be given in lipreading and the making of sounds as a foundation for speech. Any baby who does not seem to be responding normally to sound should be "screened" for deafness by a specially trained health visitor, and receive follow-up tests later. A hearing aid for a small child is available under National Health, but in addition parents will want to contact the National Deaf Children's Society for counselling as to how best such a child should be brought up.

At home, things "happen" to a young deaf child with terrifying suddenness. He cannot know that the tinkle of plates means food, or the running of the water means bath time — he cannot even be prepared, by hearing his mother's footsteps, for being picked up out of his cot. Later, he cannot be told when a new baby is expected, or when he is going away for a holiday, or what father does when he goes out each morning and comes home each night. He needs to be helped to grasp all this by facial expressions and gestures, and to learn that objects have names, and things you want have to be asked for. Special nursery schools for the deaf, of which there are a few, can help him enormously, and many nursery groups will admit a partially-hearing or deaf child on the recommendation of a doctor. An older child can either receive teaching at home, or attend one of the partial-hearing units (if he is lucky) attached to a local primary school, which are increasing in number from year to year. There are special day and boarding schools also for the deaf, at various levels up to grammar school.

Blind and partially sighted children can sometimes attend an ordinary school if special facilities are available; but there are also the National Institute for the Blind's Sunshine Homes for Babies which provide extremely useful nursery experience to give confidence at an early age. It is amazing to find how independent a small blind child can become, in an environment where he can play safely, negotiate steps and passages, and enjoy games and "adventure playground" activities. Blind children can obtain home teaching, but there are also special units and schools where trained teachers can care for them, and braille, "talking books" and special typewriters are available.

Physically handicapped children have many varieties of educational institutions open to them: schools for the delicate, needing open air or seaside facilities; schools for the asthmatic, the epileptic, heart cases and diabetics. In the latter case, the Church of England Children's Society has been particularly forward looking in establishing hostels where children are taught to regulate their diet and inject themselves while attending local schools. It may surprise parents to learn that there are five and a half thousand young diabetics — about one in every 1200 children — all of whom need constant care and supervision; but they can be trained to cope with their disability if help is given at an early age.

Cerebral palsied children — or spastics, as they are usually known, though this is only one form of the disability — come into the world at the rate of at least a thousand each year. They have more than a hundred schools and centres, mainly due to the efforts of the Spastics Society. Most are all-age schools for children from 5 to 16 (the leaving age for most special schools) but there are a few secondary grammar schools, and some for slow learning pupils, including the multiply-handicapped and partially hearing.

In Cambridgeshire there is an experimental training school for the worst handicapped of all spastics, the subnormal, which is producing remarkable results with children formerly considered ineducable. Here I have seen children who would never, in the old days, have become even remotely independent, learning to feed and dress themselves, enjoy simple games, and even count and paint. The exceptional success of this centre is due to the fact that it is a centre for research and discussion as well as a school. Parents and families are welcome to come and stay there, and there is a friendly liaison with the local community which is a great help to both children and staff.

Lately, at Fitzroy Square in London, a Family Services and Assessment Centre has been opened (also with facilities for families to come and stay) where children are assessed and treatment considered. Some are sent on from here for a longer period of assessment at a centre in Yorkshire, so that the best type of education can be planned for them.

Speech disorders have been one of the least recognized of physical disabilities. At present there are only two residential schools for the speech-impaired, the John Horniman School at Worthing and Moor House at Oxted; a third is planned. Many young children have a phase of "stumbling" speech akin to the stumbling manner in which they begin to walk, but if they are allowed, as in walking, to pick themselves up without comment, they usually develop normal speech. However, if a child still stumbles, or stammers, or cannot get out word sounds, as school time approaches, advice must be sought.

A child with dyslalia or imperfect speech at five will probably be seen first by the school doctor, and in these cases it is often the parents who need the therapy — to be taught how to improve his speech without creating tension. About nine infant schools in England have special teaching units for groups of ten or so with severe speech disorders, or aphasics who cannot get out the words at all. The Association for All Speech Impaired Children (Afasic) has recently been formed to help worried parents and children, and will give counselling as to the best form of education, and of course the school speech therapist will help.

Aphasia — where children hear but do not talk — must be diagnosed early, at least by four and a half, and deafness as a possibility first eliminated. But with most of these children the best therapy is relaxation: fun and games, which lead to speech imperceptibly, puppets, dressing-up, singing, accompanied by skilled teaching which turns the "enemy" speech into a friend. With older children a tape recorder is useful, and the new invention the Language Master, which makes speech into a game. Things to do with other children which don't involve speech, or which get a child to "speak" through another medium such as a make believe character in an improvised play, help him to integrate into the community.

A further category of the handicapped which has only recently come to light is the word blind or dyslexic. Here, a child has difficulty in reading and writing, because of a brain disorder which makes him unable to recognize quite ordinary words. Some 20 per cent of children have reading or writing problems, but only a very few of these are really dyslexic — strangely, a proportion of four boys to one girl. The attainments of these often intelligent children fall far below what one would expect; as one teacher of a dyslexic little girl put it, "her written work is just rubbish, but she has such wonderful ideas!"

The dyslexic sees every word, as it were, for the first time, and so repeats himself and loses the place in reading; he cannot start a new line when it comes to writing, and in drawing he may squeeze all his work into a tiny corner, being unable to utilize space. His spelling is quite bizarre, and he often reverses the letters he writes. Since 1959 the Department of Education and Science has recognized this condition, and allows local authorities to pay for remedial treatment.

Parents can help by trying to teach the sounds of words rather than their shapes. It is the phonetic method which helps the dyslexic reader. He must also be helped to manage direction and space — concepts which are difficult for him. In some districts skilled teachers are able to cope with the dyslexic; or there may·

be a hospital clinic. In London, the Word Blind Centre, set up
for research into this condition, and the only place of its kind in
this country, has now had to close; though Copenhagen, in contrast, has had such a centre for more than thirty years.

Pioneers in helping the dyslexic have been the Invalid
Children's Aid Association, which established the centre and
which issues regular bulletins for teachers and parents. This
Association in fact is one of the best known societies for helping
all handicapped and delicate children, advising on problems,
providing numerous practical aids, escorting children to and
from boarding schools, and running holiday centres of its own
for those with specific handicaps.

Hospitalized children

Supposing your normally healthy child becomes ill and has to go
to hospital? Many parents worry about this; hospital confine-
ment is bad enough, but any prolonged absence from home and
school can set a child back seriously, especially if it comes at a
critical time such as the beginning of infant school or the change
from infants to juniors.

There is, however, a well organized teaching service for the
children's wards in most hospitals. At the pre-school stage, this
may be a nursery nurse or a "play lady" who keeps the under-
fives busy and cheerful, and in contact with the world outside.
This is not only a great aid to recovery, but a vital necessity for
a child who will shortly have to adapt himself to school.

For school-age patients, the hospital teacher finds occupations which are not too demanding, and continues, where possible,
the work a child is doing in class. Some hospitals have special
playrooms and schoolrooms where "lessons" and creative
activities can go on for young convalescents. Other children
have to manage in bed. If, on return, a child is still not well
enough to go back to school, the authority can provide a home
tutor to give lessons either in the child's home or in her own,
and this is a great help in bridging the gap between hospital and
school life.

Home teaching

If a child under special circumstances can be taught by a tutor at
home, can a mother do this herself? This is a question which does

arise from time to time, where a family is very isolated with no suitable school within reach, or, in the early years, where a father's job keeps him constantly on the move. And of course it applies especially to young children who are living with their parents overseas.

There is an answer to this problem — the Parents' National Educational Union, which is a "home school" based on the principles of a very progressive nineteenth century teacher, Charlotte Mason, who was well ahead of her time in her views on education for young children. The organization she founded, besides running certain schools of its own in this country, has about 28 independent overseas schools, and also organizes a correspondence course which enables parents to teach young children at home.

Thousands of mothers have, over the years, received from the PNEU a properly planned correspondence course, together with the use of the library when they are in London, and a monthly journal which keeps families in touch with what is going on in the educational world. The ten to twenty pound annual fee per child (with a reduction for more than one child) for home tuition covers lessons from the ages of five to eleven, and there is a pre-school teaching booklet "The First Five Years." Children take exams twice yearly, there are the usual terms, and school hours of course have to be strictly observed in a programme which is to take the place of regular school attendance.

Parents abroad

Should a child living abroad start at the local school? Many parents find that the local nursery school in most countries is perfectly satisfactory for a young child; but after seven, school systems vary so much that they may prove obstacles to a child's learning, especially if the family is often on the move. For the Services there are Forces schools all over the world. It is a useful thing for parents to remember that other families besides Service ones can sometimes get places for children at these schools if they are willing to pay fees.

In this country, however, there are very few provisions for primary children to be educated when their parents are abroad. Only one or two authorities have hostels for a handful of younger children who attend a local day school. State secondary schools, however, do provide certain boarding places, or hostels where children can live; it is important, here, for parents to make enquiries in good time, and also, where possible, to find a base in this country — either with relatives or with friends, or possibly even with foster parents — for a child about to start secondary schooling, as the home where a child lives over here will determine which local authority will later help with boarding facilities.

Of course there are many private boarding schools catering especially or mainly for children with parents abroad, and organizing their holidays where necessary. But all these need the most careful vetting. In exceptional cases a local authority may help with fees at such a school, and it is worth making enquiries if you feel that one particular school would be best for your child, or if older brothers or sisters are already there.

Parents abroad would do well to get an independent assessment of a child's attainments when he is about eleven, as often, when he comes back to this country to take the test normally given to children here, he does not show his abilities to the full. An educational psychologist can be consulted, abroad or in London, and his report will be taken into consideration when it comes to finding a suitable school for the secondary stage.

Boarding school for your child?

Can local authorities help with boarding fees where a family wishes a child of primary age to go away from home? Many parents would like to know the answer to this question, but the issues are very complicated. On the one hand, local authorities are usually reluctant to pay fees simply for boarding education where a suitable day school already exists. On the other hand, some parents who have proved real need have been able to get help — largely through knowing their parental rights and having a great deal of perseverance.

Where parents are divorced, or where there is excessive family stress owing, perhaps, to illness or mental instability at home, or where the mother is the sole support and is obliged to go out to work, a case might well be made out for boarding education. There would also be a call for it where a family is constantly on the move, or where there is a disjointed home life: in one case, a little girl had periodically to go and live with her grandmother, changing schools every time, because her mother had to go to hospital. It is always worth trying to get financial aid where circumstances like these prevail, but much depends on the locality in which you happen to live.

There are a limited number of State boarding schools for over elevens; and certain independent schools are recognized as providing a rather special type of education for younger children — such as the Rudolf Steiner schools, the Quaker schools, and some Direct Grant schools with a boarding hostel attached. For these, a parent could consult books in the reference department of the local library, or ask for an appointment with the Director of Education.

One way or another, there are vast numbers of "special" children with needs which cannot be met simply by sending them to the school around the corner. Such cases require careful thought, for it is most important that "special" children, in spite of their circumstances, should not be led to feel themselves different from others. The more they can be integrated into the community, the better; in fact, recent research has consistently shown that their development is very closely linked to the way they are welcomed into and accepted by family, neighbours and friends.

Many children go through periods of special stress; others will always be mentally or physically "special." But even these like to think of themselves, as one heavily handicapped little girl once told me, as "not special but ordinary." The sooner we include them with ordinary children, acknowledging only their greater need for friendship and help, the better they will get on, not only learning but being happy — which is what we want for all our children everywhere.

Index

Index

Some useful addresses

Abbatt, Paul and Marjorie, 94 Wimpole Street, London W1
Advisory Centre for Education, 32 Trumpington Street, Cambridge (ACE)
Association for All Speech Impaired Children, Hon Sec Mrs J Rankin, 9 Desenfans
 Road, Dulwich Village, London SE21 (Afasic)
Children's Book Centre, 140 Kensington Church Street, London W8
Choir Schools Association, The Cathedral Choir School, Ripon, Yorks
Confederation for the Advancement of State Education, Sec Mrs B. Bullivant,
 81 Rustlings Road, Sheffield (CASE)
Educational Supply Association, 179 Tottenham Court Road, London W1
Friends' Schools, Friends' Education Council, Friends' House, Euston Road, London N
Galt Toys, 30 Great Marlborough Street, London W1
Home and School Council (representing ACE, CASE and PTA's), joint secs
 John Hale, Shears Green Junior School, White Avenue, Northfleet, Gravesend,
 Kent *and* Mrs B. Bullivant, 81 Rustlings Road, Sheffield
Invalid Children's Aid Association, 126 Buckingham Palace Road, London SW1
National Association for Gifted Children, 21 Montagu Street, London W1
National Book League, 7 Albemarle Street, London W1
National Confederation of Parent-Teacher Associations, 127 Herbert Gdns.,
 London NW10
National Deaf Children's Society, 31 Gloucester Place, London W1
National Extension College, 32 Trumpington Street, Cambridge
National Society for Autistic Children, 1a Golders Green Road, London NW11
National Society for Mentally Handicapped Children, 5 Bulstrode Street, London W1
Nursery School Association, 89 Stamford Street, London SE1
Parents' National Educational Union, Murray House, Vandon Street, London SW1
Playcraft, Sutherland House, 5 Argyll Street, London W1
Pre-school Playgroups Association, 87a Borough High Street, London SE1
Quaker Schools, see Friends' Schools
Royal National Institute for the Blind, 224 Great Portland Street, London W1
Rudolf Steiner Schools, 38 Museum Street, London WC1
Rural Music Schools Association, Little Benslow Hills, Hitchin, Herts
Save the Children Fund, 29 Queen Anne's Gate, London SW1
Spastics Society, 12 Park Crescent, London W1
Society of Teachers Opposed to Physical Punishment, 12 Lawn Road, London NW3
 (Stopp)
Wood, Mrs Anne, 100 Church Lane East, Aldershot